Jazz

Tenth Edition

Paul O. W. Tanner
University of California
Los Angeles

David W. Megill
MiraCosta College

Maurice Gerow
University of California
Los Angeles

Mc Graw Hill

Boston Burr Ridge, IL Dubuque, IA Madison, WI New York
San Francisco St. Louis Bangkok Bogotá Caracas Kuala Lumpur
Lisbon London Madrid Mexico City Milan Montreal New Delhi
Santiago Seoul Singapore Sydney Taipei Toronto

The McGraw-Hill Companies

Higher Education

Jazz, Tenth Edition

Published by McGraw-Hill, an imprint of The McGraw-Hill Companies, Inc., 1221 Avenue of the Americas, New York, NY 10020.

1 2 3 4 5 6 7 8 9 0 VNH / VNH 0 9 8 7 6 5 4

ISBN 0-07-294543-5

Publisher: *Lyn Uhl*
Senior sponsoring editor: *Melody Marcus*
Developmental editor: *Nadia Bidwell*
Editorial assistant: *Beth Ebenstein*
Marketing manager: *Lisa Berry*
Senior media producer: *Todd Vaccaro*
Media supplement producer: *Meghan Durko*
Production editor: *Brett Coker*
Production supervisor: *Tandra Jorgensen*
Design manager and cover designer: *Preston Thomas*
Interior designer: *Mark Ong*
Art editor: *Cristin Yancey*
Photo research coordinator: *Natalia Peschiera*
Photo researcher: *Connie Gardner*
Cover illustration: *Robin Shepherd © Super Stock*
Compositor: *Professional Graphics*
Typeface: *10/12 Meridien Roman*
Paper: *45# Publishers Matte*
Printer and binder: *Von Hoffmann Press*

Library of Congress Cataloging-in-Publication Data

Tanner, Paul, 1917-
Jazz / Paul O.W. Tanner, David W. Megill, Maurice Gerow.—10th ed.
p. cm.
Includes bibliographical references and index.
ISBN 0-07-294543-5
1. Jazz—History and criticism. I. Megill, David W. II. Gerow, Maurice.

ML3506.T36 2004
781.65'09—dc22

2004042571

www.mhhe.com

Preface

We designed this new edition of *Jazz* to offer students a listening-based approach to the evolutionary development of America's unique art form. We have increased the number of musical selections to offer a more comprehensive overview of important musical performances that anchor our historical overview. This edition is also meant to support instructors in their individual approaches to the jazz experience. Comprehensive citations to additional listening are given throughout the text. A new, interactive CD-ROM accompanies the book and provides numerous enrichment activities to accompany the readings in addition to stylistic musical examples.

CHANGES TO THE TENTH EDITION

- Beautiful, **four-color design** throughout the text
- A **free Multimedia Companion CD-ROM** now accompanies every new copy of the book purchased from McGraw-Hill. Features include the following:
  - Demonstration recordings illustrating jazz styles
  - Instrument film clips
  - Flashcards testing knowledge of key terms
  - Timelines
  - Matching quizzes
- **Vocal jazz coverage** is now integrated throughout the presentation where appropriate.
- A **third audio CD** with additional jazz recordings is now available for separate purchase.
- The new, text-specific **Online Learning Center** provides a wealth of additional resources such as listening software for use with the audio CDs, multiple-choice quizzes, enhanced coverage of jazz around the world, and links to useful websites.

SPECIAL FEATURES

- **"Witness to Jazz":** A series of essays featuring the images of renowned journalist/photographer William Gottlieb conveys personal anecdotes about musicians such as Dizzy Gillespie, Mary Lou Williams, and Louis Armstrong.
- **"Profiles in Jazz":** Biographical sketches highlight key figures from the jazz community.
- **"Vamping":** Interesting asides interspersed throughout the text add color to the presentation and enhance student understanding of the world of jazz.
- **Effective Learning Tools:** Summaries, suggestions for further study/listening/reading, and listening guides provide students with extensive support to master the material and enhance their knowledge of jazz.
- For those students with some musical training, we offer **optional material in the appendix** that includes notated musical examples and more advanced theoretical discussions.

We offer additional listening guides in the text for selections found on the *Smithsonian Collection of Classic Jazz.* An "S" identifies examples from this collection when they appear in the text. References are also made to the New World Records' collection and are identified by "NW." This collection can be obtained from 3 East 54th St., New York, New York 10022. Some references are also made to the Folkways Jazz series, identified by "FJ."

The primary author of the text, Paul Tanner, who was the lead trombonist for the Glenn Miller band and the first educator to introduce jazz studies in higher education at U.C.L.A., offers some personal insights throughout the volume. You may also correspond directly with the author on the Internet at *dwmegill@miracosta.edu.*

RECORDINGS

Three audio CDs are now available. In addition to the 2-CD set (0-07-294544-3), there is now a third audio CD (0-07-304891-7) with additional jazz tracks available for separate purchase. All of the selections on each audio CD have a companion listening guide in the text.

SUPPORT FOR INSTRUCTORS

For the instructor, we offer an Instructor's Resource CD-ROM (0-07-294547-8) that includes the following elements:

- Instructor's manual with musical scores of the stylistic examples on the CD-ROM
- Test bank
- Computerized Test Bank
- PowerPoint slides.

SUPPORT FOR STUDENTS

A text-specific Online Learning Center at **www.mhhe.com/jazz10** is available for students, which offers learning materials to help underpin the reading as well as supplemental activities for personal and classroom use. These activities include multiple-choice quizzes, links to useful websites, and many additional resources. Interactive listening software is available from this site that guides listeners through the musical selections referenced in the text and found on the audio CDs.

Jazz is a history of individuals connected to their culture through their musical art. Jazz is a wonderful reflector of the cultural crosscurrents at work in America. When we study jazz, we also study our own cultural development. As we unfold the rich history of jazz, we hope that we will also connect you to the vitality of the American voice heard so clearly in the performances presented here.

ACKNOWLEDGMENTS

This book could not have been written without the careful manuscript reviews by a number of professors. I would like to thank Scott Cowan, Western Michigan University; Larry Dwyer, University of Notre Dame; John Fremgen, University of Texas Austin; Peter Janson, University of Massachusetts Boston; Gary Langford, University of Florida; Chris Merz, University of Northern Iowa; Doug Reid, Shoreline Community College; Marc Rice, Truman State University; Andrew Speight, San Francisco State University; David Such, Spokane Community College.

Contents

5 EARLY NEW ORLEANS AND CHICAGO STYLE JAZZ 87

6 SWING 117

7 DUKE ELLINGTON 159

8 BOP 177

9 COOL/THIRD STREAM 203

10 MILES DAVIS 225

11 HARD BOP, FUNKY, GOSPEL JAZZ 239

12 FREE FORM, AVANT-GARDE 261

13 JAZZ/ROCK FUSION 287

14 CONTEMPORARY TRENDS: A MATURING ART FORM 313

15 LATIN JAZZ 339

Recorded Demonstrations

Jazz

1

Listening to Jazz

> *"Jazz is considered by many to be America's greatest contribution to music. Its impact on American society has been enormous and its influence on world culture has been far reaching. Its message has been direct, vital, and immediate, enabling it to hurdle cultural, linguistic, and political barriers."*[1]
>
> Robert Hickok

AN OVERVIEW

Throughout its chronology, jazz has freely imported influences from diverse cultural and musical elements, forming a type of music that has been accepted as uniquely American. "The American popular song is inextricably and profoundly linked with jazz, the one serving—along with the blues—as the basic melodic/harmonic material on which the other could build."[2]

Jazz is both indigenous to this country and the most democratic music ever to evolve. Performers in an improvised jazz ensemble are equal partners in the developing musical expression. As the music unfolds, the musical leadership may shift several times as the players contribute their own expressive ideas. Jazz is defined by this balance between the individual voices that constitute an ensemble and the collective expression unique to that ensemble.

In its early development, all music not clearly classical was generally considered jazz, thereby putting jazz, country and western, rock and roll, and all popular and other types of music into one category. As jazz developed, the lines between it and the other musics in America became much clearer. In fact, even the distinction between "good" and "bad" jazz seems to have settled into a general consensus, but this consensus has seldom developed free of controversy.

The music of America has many faces. Few of these musical expressions survive a temporary popularity, but jazz ultimately matured in a way that wove it into the American fabric itself. It is often called "America's classical music," and it has proven to be an appropriate subject of study in colleges and universities around the world. Although there was other musical activity during this time—such as country and western, blues, rhythm and blues, and the popular songs of musical theater—jazz was the first to claim a dominant foothold in the American identity.

This musical and cultural phenomenon was not to be replicated until the advent of rock and roll, which now appears to have an equal amount of cultural energy to etch itself, as jazz did, into the American identity. Jazz embodies the irony of how a music can move from such lowly origins as the heartfelt expressions of American slaves, the music of the church, and the dance hall to the American academy and the concert stage.

Birdland, 1949: Max Kaminsky, Lester Young, George Wettling, Hot Lips Page, and Charlie Parker

When jazz first took shape, players did not foresee its acceptance as an art form. If this fact had been known, perhaps better records would have been kept of just how the transformation occurred. Jazz coalesced out of the many diverse musical influences present at the turn of the century. It is a music that could have developed only in the United States. It required all the elements, good and bad. It needed the rich African oral tradition of the Negro slave culture and the formal schooling practices inherited from the Western European musical tradition. It needed the urban and rural folk music as well as the white and black church music practices. It needed the songs of **Tin Pan Alley,** the "Roaring Twenties," the marching bands, the jug bands, the tenderloins, the blues, the religious fervor of the Great Awakening, the hopelessness of slavery. Without all of these elements, the recipe for jazz would have been incomplete and not the American expression it is today.

HISTORICAL FRAME OF REFERENCE

Trying to recreate the actual blend of musical cultures from which jazz emerged leaves a great deal to speculation. The musical examples we do have are limited by the recording capabilities of the time, and these examples often stand stripped of the cultural associations that they reflected. To describe the music, the written accounts tend to use a theoretical system that is tailored to European classical music, a literate system that is significantly limited when applied to music that developed from an oral tradition. Consequently, we cannot notate the expressive singing style typical of the musically nonliterate practice at that time.

Without appropriate notation and audio recordings, only written descriptions are available. Like all historical accounts these documentations tend to reflect the dominant cultural view. The language of the descriptions often reflects a frame of reference external to the musical culture being described. Such a report from the outside would tend to overlook potentially important nonmusical associations significant to the inside participants. What did the expressive church music mean to the enslaved black? How was jazz influenced by the strong emotional crosscurrents of the Civil Rights movement? From a distance, such cultural forces may unfortunately lose much of their significance. As we look at the substance of the music, we must also strive to place it in a framework that reveals its meaning.

UNDERSTANDING JAZZ

Understanding jazz requires an understanding of the jazz performer. Unlike music of the Western European tradition, which traces the history of musical composition, jazz traces its history through the performance of individuals. Jazz is about personal, unique expressions, and those performers most remembered by history have always stood above others in the power of their personal expressions. These expressions have always depended on the unique balance of the technical and aesthetic prowess of the performers themselves.

Witness to Jazz

Mary Lou's Salon

Photo and text by William P. Gottlieb. Bill Gottlieb stopped taking jazz photos in 1948; but, in 1979, after retiring, he began an intensive involvement with those old, now classic images. Several of these images are featured in this text accompanied by his personal comments. Gottlieb received the jazz photography "Oscar" of 1999 at the Bell Atlantic Festival in New York. In 1997 he received the annual *Down Beat* Magazine Lifetime Achievement Award, the first given to a photographer.

"The all-time greatest woman jazz musician!" That's a typical description of Mary Lou Williams. Mary Lou was, beyond dispute, a fabulous pianist, as well as a noted arranger and composer.

She also had another role of distinction: that of a sort of "mother spirit" for musicians. Her spacious Harlem apartment was a "salon" where, in the 1940s, many prominent jazz people hung out, especially—though not exclusively—those musicians whose style was at the cutting edge.

I was a friend of Mary Lou and particularly remember when, in 1947, she had me show up at her place for an evening gathering. The turnout was small but choice. Among the group that appeared were three disparate geniuses who were, or became, members of the *Down Beat* magazine "Hall of Fame": Dizzy Gillespie, the trumpeter and bebop icon; Jack Teagarden, the premier trombonist of the era; and Mary Lou, herself. To top it off, there were two of the most prominent boppers: pianist–arranger Tadd Dameron, and pianist Hank Jones.

It was a serious social gathering. No jamming. Just serious talk, mostly *about* music . . . with some attention to recordings played on Mary Lou's small phonograph and occasional moments at a piano by one or another of the guests to illustrate a point. As for the usually flamboyant Dizzy, he had no horn but smoked a pipe, looking on as if he were an elder statesman. The hostess, for her part, was all dressed up, with a corsage pinned to her dress.

A memorable evening!

Because jazz is defined by the personal voices of its performers and only secondarily by its composers, it is misleading to force the musical styles used to define jazz into overly rigid categories. The stylistic similarities among players of a particular era are useful in understanding the evolution of jazz, but they are only a shadow of the individual creative voices that propelled jazz's evolution.

An important first step to understanding jazz is recognizing that jazz is not static within its own tradition. This must be established before trying to distinguish it from the other musical traditions in America, a task that at first seems obvious but that ultimately proves more elusive than one would expect. What characteristics are common to almost all jazz and are not typical of other musical traditions? It is much easier to recognize something as jazz than to state how one knows it is jazz and not something else. The more technical musical activities understood only by the practitioners of music somehow signal to even the untrained listener that it is jazz rather than some other musical style. Actually, the musical elements of jazz are very similar to those used in other musical styles. Also, most of the musical forms (or structures) of jazz are not new to American music. However, jazz is still recognizably different, its most distinctive attribute being the manner in which all these elements and forms are performed and the improvised context in which this jazz interpretation is carried out.

The interpretation of music in the jazz style originally came about when African Americans attempted to express themselves on European musical instruments. These early instrumentalists tended to think of their musical lines in terms of how they would be treated vocally. Eventually, the attitude developed that *what* was played was not as important as *how* it was played.

In jazz interpretation, the player restricts interpretative ideas to his or her conception of the melody, coloring it with the use of rhythmic effects, dynamics, and any other slight alterations that occur to him or her while performing. The player remains enough within such melodic restrictions to allow a listener to recognize the melody easily, regardless of the player's interpretation. Almost any kind of melodic line can be performed with jazz interpretation. Most jazz musicians will agree that to write down an exact jazz interpretation is next to impossible, and all will agree that only a musician who has played jazz can even approximate the notation.

WHAT TO LISTEN FOR IN JAZZ

> "There need be no mystery about jazz, but each listener has a right, even a duty, to be discriminating."[3]

To appreciate music, the listener must be actively involved, and understanding and enjoyment go hand in hand. Passive listening will not bring intelligent musical enjoyment. Rather, such enjoyment is fostered through active participation that includes understanding, careful listening, and emotional response. The thrust of all musical learning should be to develop a sensitized awareness of those expressive elements of music that will foster a wide range of musical interests and activities and a variety of musical pleasures.

The primary aim in listening to a composition is to focus attention on the various musical events as they unfold—not an easy task. Mental concentration of a high order is needed. The mind is so conditioned to hearing music as a background **accompaniment** to daily activities—in the dentist's office or at the supermarket—that it is difficult to devote full attention to listening to music.

In daily living, one encounters many spatial relationships—high walls and low walls, houses and garages, sidewalks and streets, country and urban vistas—that are immediately visual and easily identified. In listening to music, one must forget the visual and learn to concentrate on the nonvisual elements.

Another difference is that music moves in time, and time relationships are less obvious in daily living. For example, a painting can be viewed at leisure and its parts observed in relationship to the whole, but not so when listening to a musical composition, when memory becomes important. The mind must remember at one point what has transpired so that one part of a piece of music can be compared or contrasted with another part.

Finally, if one is to learn more about the structure of music, it is important to develop the ability to separate juxtaposed musical sounds and to focus attention on a single musical element. For example, when identifying the **ostinato** bass employed in boogie-woogie playing, one must be able to shut out the right-hand piano sounds to recognize what the left hand is realizing at the keyboard.

Sounds Associated with Jazz

In classical music, each instrument has an "ideal" sound or tone, or at least there is a consensus as to what the ideal sound is. The jazz musician, though, finds such conformity of little importance. As long as the sound communicates well with peers and listeners, the jazz musician appreciates the individuality of personal sounds. This situation, in which personal expression is more important than aesthetic conformity, often causes listeners not accustomed to jazz to question the sounds that they hear.

Certain sounds peculiar to jazz have their origins in oral tradition and are the result of instrumentalists attempting to imitate vocal techniques. Jazz singers and instrumentalists use all the tone qualities employed in other music and even increase the emotional range through the use of growls, bends, slurs, and varying shades of **vibrato,** employing any device they can to assist their personal interpretation of the music. Jazz musicians have always had a great affinity with good singers, especially those whose interpretation closely resembles their own. Such singers include the early great blues singers (to be discussed later) and other talented performers such as Bing Crosby, Ella Fitzgerald, Billie Holiday, Frank Sinatra, Sarah Vaughan, Billy Eckstine, and Betty Carter.

Distinctive jazz **instrumentation** produces unique sounds. For example, a featured saxophone section or a **rhythm section** is seldom found in other types of music. Although it is a mistake to claim that mutes are indigenous to

Sarah Vaughan
Courtesy of Ray Avery

jazz (mutes were used in the 1600s), it is true that a larger variety of mutes are used in jazz.

To many listeners, the sounds of jazz are personified and identified through the musical interpretation of specific artists. Listeners who have not heard much jazz are often surprised that the well-initiated can recognize a soloist after hearing only a few notes—at least within the listener's preferred style. Talented jazz musicians seem to have their own personal vibrato, attack, type of melodic line, choice of notes in the **chord**—indeed, their own sound. On the other hand, very few classical connoisseurs can say for sure who is conducting a standard work, let alone identify the individual soloists or section leaders.

Listen to the recorded demonstrations to hear how a classically played melody (demonstration 1) can be given a jazz interpretation (demonstration 2). Demonstration 3 then offers a possible improvisation of that same melody.

Improvisation and Composition

What is the jazz "idiom"? Classical music and jazz music differ primarily in idiom. A classical musician plays the notes, but the playing lacks the idiomatic execution usually found in jazz. The European system of musical notation cannot represent this kind of expression. "The conventional symbols could, in other words, indicate in a general way *what* should be played, but could not indicate *how* it should be played."[4] Idiomatic expression in jazz is the result of African American musicians interjecting African music into European music.

The Western European musical tradition is a history of literate composition. We study it through whatever written music remains from early musical periods. Without recordings, all that remains is the notation itself or descriptions of musical practice. This shortcoming no doubt influences the way we study Western European music. The African American oral tradition is a history of performers and performances. How the music is played is more important than how the music was composed. Fortunately, jazz history is relatively recent and there are recordings to help us understand the true musical practice of most styles.

A jazz composition can strike any number of balances between improvisation and composition:

1. The most composed composition is completely notated and the performer(s) is expected to play exactly what is written. An example might be the way a member of the trumpet section of a big swing band would be expected to play his part.
2. The performer(s) may play a melody that is an accurate reflection of the notation but place a distinctive interpretive style by bending notes, adding vibrato, altering the rhythm, etc. An example might be the way a blues singer sings a familiar melody.
3. The performer may make so many changes in the melody that it is barely recognizable. Swing soloists often made use of this type of improvisation. This type of improvisation would not be written by the composer but rather created by the performer.
4. The performer may play over the chords of a song but not try to include any of the given melody at all. In this case, there would be no written melody—it would be created entirely by the performer.
5. The performer(s) may create the entire musical performance without any reference to a known musical melody or composition. The free jazz players often improvise everything with no previously known chords or melody.
6. Performers can improvise "collectively" to create new musical performances. All the players in a group make up their own parts and little or no notation is needed. All the levels of improvisation mentioned above can be used to improvise collectively. For example, the Early New Orleans ensembles created their music by improvising all the parts, while arrangements written for the big bands, like those of Benny Goodman or Glenn Miller, might be completely composed in advance, expecting only the drummer and guitarist to improvise their parts.

The development of jazz can be viewed as a balancing act between the literate tradition of composition and the oral tradition of **improvisation.** These two dominant forces in jazz emanate from the ethnic groups that have contributed to the developing art form, in particular, the African Americans and the Western Europeans. Each of these large groups carries sensitivities and preferences that play themselves out in the way each approaches the writing and performing of jazz. Depending on which influence is dominant at any one time, jazz has changed to reflect that influence. This balance is quite unstable and has shifted dramatically from the inception of jazz to the present.

If forced to reduce the contrast between the artistic approaches of the African American and Western European cultures to a single theme, one might consider the African American influence to be one of an oral tradition that expresses itself in the improvisatory actions of performance as contrasted to the literate tradition of Western European compositional practice. The exceptions to this very general statement are many and obvious. However, this distinction proves to be quite useful for tracing an evolutionary line through jazz that describes the influence of these two cultures.

It may be useful as you study the musical jazz periods to identify the balance between these musical forces. Some jazz styles tip the scales strongly in one direction while others show a careful balance. Of course, even within a stylistic period different performers strike their own balance. The Western European contributions to jazz often emerge most clearly in those stylistic periods where composition is stressed (cool, third stream, early jazz/rock, the theoretical side of avant-garde, and fusion). These styles form an identifiable evolutionary thread that is interwoven with a parallel thread that is more typical of the African American oral tradition that stresses improvisation (Early New Orleans, bop, hard bop, the free side of avant-garde, mainstream).

As you will see in later chapters, it was Duke Ellington who best controlled the balance between improvisation and composition. His compositions exhibited a complexity that an edited compositional approach affords while maintaining room within the architecture of the composition for the rich and individual improvisational voices of the members of his ensembles.

Rhythm—Syncopation

"Rhythm is the most magnetic irresistible force among all the elements of music."[5]

An emphasis on rhythm has always been an integral part of jazz, one reason being that for many years jazz was considered primarily dance music. Jazz players have found that a steady, unbroken beat is necessary not only for dancing but also for developing the emotional pitch identified with jazz, even though in some cases the pulse is merely implied rather than obvious.

The jazz player does not always play exactly in rhythm with the pulse. He or she sometimes feels the need to be slightly ahead of (on top of) the beat and sometimes to be slightly behind the beat **(lay back).** This is more a feeling than something that can be measured accurately, and it varies from one style and from one individual to another. Throughout the development of most jazz, performers have felt that they needed this pulse to play what they considered jazz. However, recent experiments in jazz have not used a steady beat. (These experiments in rhythm are discussed further in Chapter 12.) For years it was thought that all jazz must be played with a steady beat, but this attitude changed when

Paul Desmond
Lee Tanner/The Jazz Image

new, uneven-beat groups **(meters)** began to be used in performing well-accepted jazz works. Pianist Dave Brubeck first brought newer meters to public notice with an extremely popular recording of Paul Desmond's "Take Five."[6] Most jazz, however, still uses even meters.

Jazz also makes use of a specific type of rhythmic treatment called **syncopation,** which places accents between the basic beats in the music. Jazz uses this so much that it has become one of its identifying characteristics. Syncopation is responsible to a great extent for the "swing feel" most often associated with jazz.

Syncopation and Swing

Tap your foot as you listen to a jazz selection and listen for notes that fall between the taps. These notes in jazz are often accented for emphasis. When the notes between the beats are accented more than the notes on the beat, a syncopated style is created. These syncopated notes also determine how much swing the music has. As you listen you may notice that the notes do not always fall exactly between each of the beats. Often the notes in the middle of the beats are moved back in time toward the beat that follows them. The combination of the delayed notes and their **accents** give the performance its swing. Some styles like bop swing more (or harder) than others like cool. This swing is considered by many to be an essential ingredient in jazz, although we will find that some jazz styles have very little swing while others are characterized by it.

Form

The word **form** in music describes the overall structure of a musical composition or performance. Perceiving and understanding the elements of form present a greater challenge in listening to music than in considering visual art. In

Vamping

Degrees of Swing

Actually, it is quite natural to swing a melody. One only has to listen to children on a playground tease one another to hear a very common and natural swing. For example, the tease you might hear is "Suzie has a boyfriend," which is sung in a melody most everyone knows. Children naturally swing this melody. You can experiment with this melody to create different degrees of swing. First tap your foot while you sing Su-uzie has a boy friend. The syllables not underscored fall between the beats and are the notes that create the swing.

1. First sing the melody with the notes exactly in the middle between the beats. This should feel stiff with little or no swing. Even children swing it more than this.
2. Keep the notes exactly in the middle between the beats but now put an accent on them so that "zie" and "a" are louder than the surrounding syllables. You should begin to feel a swing develop. This is the type of swing found most in jazz ballads.
3. Now delay the notes in the middle so they come just before the next beat keeping the accents. This should create a stronger sense of swing that is more typical of faster swing or bop performances.
4. Experiment with the placement and accent of the middle notes to create different amounts of swing.

As you can see, how much swing a performer uses can be personal and quite individual. It is interesting that the amount of swing used can vary geographically. Often the more relaxed West Coast Swing is compared to the harder driving East Coast Swing. But even within these broad categories, individual performers or ensembles are characterized by the way they swing.

music, the various parts of a composition are presented in time, and a listener can compare them by memory only. Many jazz pieces have relatively simple forms, such as the blues, which have a single musical section made up of three smaller **phrases.** During the entire performance, this musical section is repeated many times.

Repetition is the presentation of the same musical material in two or more parts of a composition. **Contrast** is the introduction of different musical material. From earliest times, repetition of a melody has played a vital role in prolonging a game, dance, or story. A similar reason for repetition is found in work songs, in which repetition of the melody depends on the amount of work to be done by those singing the song. When contrasting musical ideas are introduced, a new section of the form begins. The repetitions and contrasts tend not only to build the performance but also to give a feeling of balance and symmetry to the composition as a whole. If you understand the principles of repetition and contrast, you can sharpen your listening focus by anticipating the parts that are repeated and those that are contrasted and thus will have a much better idea of what to listen to and for. Consequently, you will enjoy the music more as it unfolds.

LISTENING GUIDELINES

As you continue your study of jazz, we suggest that you concentrate on some specific points while you listen, remembering that any jazz performance can have a blend of any of the following:

1. What are the general stylistic characteristics that make the style identifiable? For example, is the music fast? Does it have a swing feel, or does it have a rock-and-roll feel? Does it seem agitated or subdued?
2. What instruments are used, and how do the instrumentalists interact? Do they work closely together in a way that would require a previously written arrangement, or do they interact spontaneously?
3. What makes the performance a personal one? Does the singer or instrumentalist use any unique tone or inflections? Are there melodic or rhythmic clues that would distinguish this performer from another? Does the performance focus more on virtuoso technique or expressive content?
4. How do the bass player, drummer, and rhythm player (guitar, piano, etc.) interact? Which has the more dominant role? How do their balance and their roles differ from other styles? How does the drummer (if present) use the drum set differently for this style?
5. What other types of music possibly influence what you are hearing? Are there any classical, rock, country, gospel, rhythm and blues, or world music influences? From what jazz style is the performance derived?
6. Is there any obvious musical form (e.g., standard song form), or are the performers also improvising the form?
7. Is the melody singable, or is it designed more appropriately for the instrument playing it? Do the melodies played or sung overlap, or are they harmonized?
8. What is the musical focus of the performance? The performer? The composition? The group as a whole?
9. What is the social context for this style? Is it a reaction to previous musical styles? Is there a social message?

For a more technical approach to listening to jazz, see Appendix A.

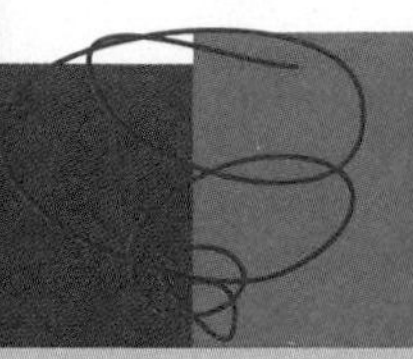

Summary

As we have seen, listening to jazz is an active endeavor that benefits from knowing the historical context of this developing art form as well as the identifying characteristics that set it aside from other styles of music. The characteristics outlined here are not present in every jazz performance. They are really only tendencies more likely to occur in a jazz performance than in other musical styles.

See Multimedia Companion for additional study materials.

1. Jazz evolution is a history of performers more than composers, although both improvisation and composition are important parts of jazz.
2. Most jazz performances have some degree of improvisation. At one extreme it may only be a freely interpreted melody, and on the other so free that no precomposed music or compositional intentions are used at all.
3. Jazz has an interpretive style that makes use of vocal and instrumental inflections or idioms less common in other styles of music.
4. Jazz performances are usually very rhythmic and syncopated and have varying amounts of swing.
5. What is played is often less important than how it is played. Performers are expected to integrate something of their own personality and background into the performance.

These are, of course, very broad in scope and it is easy to find jazz performances that may clearly avoid most traditional jazz characteristics.

FOR FURTHER STUDY

1. If you were asked to describe why you prefer a particular type of music, what would you say?
2. Listen to "Silver" from the album *Collaboration* by the Modern Jazz Quartet with Laurindo Almeida (Atlantic Records, 1429) and answer the following:
   a. Is the ensemble a large group or a small combo?
   b. See how many of the following instruments you can identify in the tune: violin, vibraphone, saxophone, oboe, piano, percussion (drums and others), string bass, and amplified guitar.
3. Listen to the Modern Jazz Quartet's rendition of the very familiar carol "God Rest Ye Merry Gentlemen" (*The Modern Jazz Quartet at Music Inn*, Atlantic Records, 1247). Describe as many of the jazz ingredients as you can, including specific instrumental sounds.
4. Benny Goodman Trio and Coleman Hawkins on saxophone use jazz interpretation and jazz improvisation in the same composition. Listen to "Body and Soul" and identify the places where you find interpretation and improvisation. Do the same with Coleman Hawkins.

NOTES

1. Robert Hickok, *Exploring Music* (Dubuque, Iowa: Wm. C. Brown, 1989), 22.
2. Gunther Schuller, *The Swing Era* (London: Oxford University Press, 1989), 5n.
3. Dom Cerulli, Burt Korall, and Mort Nasatir, *The Jazz Word* (New York: Ballantine Books, 1960), 36.
4. From Henry Pleasants, *Serious Music and All That Jazz;* 1969. Reprinted by permission of Simon & Schuster, Inc., 51.
5. Schuller, *The Swing Era,* 223.
6. Dave Brubeck Quartet, *Time Out,* Columbia Records, CL-1397, and *Time Further Out,* Columbia Records, CS-8490; Don Ellis Orchestra, *Live at Monterey,* Pacific Jazz Records, PJ-10112, and *Live in 3/4 Time,* Pacific Jazz Records, PJ-10123; Elvin Jones Quartet, "That Five-Four Bag," *The Definitive Jazz Scene,* vol. 3.

2

Jazz Heritages

"Jazz is the big brother of the blues. If a guy's playing blues like we play, he's in high school. When he starts playing jazz it's like going on to college, to a school of higher learning."[1]

B.B. King

AFRICAN AND EUROPEAN INFLUENCES

The initial contributions to the development of jazz as an art form are basically undocumented because their importance was not recognized. The country had recently finished a revolution that freed part of the population to practice religion independently of the mother country while the other part of the population was just finding its own independence from within the first. These two populations, one white and the other black, put in place the balance of forces that were to shape the jazz expression. Their separate traditions, both musical and cultural, were to establish a musical genre that would be unique in the world. However, the disparity between the two also set up a constantly shifting balance between the dominant expressions of each culture, one from Western Europe, the other from Africa. Both brought different values and needs to the musical fusion that continues to define jazz: one tradition is predominantly literate and reflects that interest in its performance practice, while the other works through an expressive language typical of the oral tradition. As these traditions met, a balance of compositional concern and spontaneous expression was set in motion that ultimately shaped jazz.

INTERPRETATION AND CONTENT

All musical styles and traditions have an interpretive system of presentation that cannot always be fully described in terms of the musical elements that make up a performance. Consider the theatrical nature of a classical music concert and compare it to the performance elements of a rock concert. The manner in which each presents their musical ingredients—harmony, rhythm, and melody—is quite different. The musical elements of both are certainly arrayed differently but remain essentially the same: both use similar scales, harmonies, and even rhythmic structures, yet the outcome of the performances is so different. These musical ingredients alone do not necessarily describe the meaning inherent in each style, much like describing the parts of a butterfly fails to reveal

W. C. Handy

the beauty of the animal. As the European and African cultures interacted to create a new music, they offered different resources that generated a new way of arranging the musical elements and expressively performing them.

Jazz, as a hybrid of musical traditions, reflects a blend of musical interpretations as well as a blend of musical elements. When looking at musical style, one is tempted to deal with the describable elements of the music and overlook the more elusive but essential expressive delivery. The problem of finding the beauty in a jazz statement is compounded by the tool set we traditionally have used to describe this beauty. This tool set is inherited from the Western European musical tradition and best describes music from that tradition. For example, the European notation system does not allow for the small pitch variations employed by jazz performers, nor does it address the subtle rhythmic delivery typical of jazz. Writing music down is useful as a compositional device but is not as important in a spontaneous improvisation. Therefore, when we try to notate an expressive oral performance, we are again pulling apart the butterfly.

Outside of the musical elements themselves, there is also the expressive context in which the elements are presented. Currently, no real language exists for describing the expressive meaning of any music, let alone that of jazz. To make matters worse, the expressive context rather than the musical substance may carry the most meaning to the average listener. Certainly, the majority of listeners do not know the complex musical jargon wielded by aficionados; but their interest in the music is still genuine. We must keep this context in mind as we examine the influences that shaped the early jazz expression.

We will also see that the balance of musical content and interpretive expression did not remain static during jazz's development. It is not uncommon in jazz for the meaningful content to reside more in the expressive nature of the music rather than in the describable substance of the music, particularly when the majority of earlier jazz's music was borrowed from other musical streams. Interpretive expressions also shift constantly as jazz responds to the needs of the day. It is this changing balance between the various social and cultural attitudes on the one hand and their relationship to the musical contents on the other that generates the continuing evolution of jazz. The fact that several cultural groups are also working with the jazz expression means that simultaneous interpretive voices may be at work in any one jazz period. Compare, for instance, the white and black bands working in the swing era or the cool and hard bop styles that existed together under the same umbrella of the jazz definition.

The scattered origins of jazz—with their companion oral and literate traditions—tend to obscure any clear lines of development toward a jazz definition because that definition is one of a shifting balance and cannot be frozen for all time. Oral traditions are messy but prove to be a definite advantage for a growing and evolving art form. They have no rational guiding force or conscious theoretical systems that keep them historically neat. They develop through practice, not theoretical planning. To impose, in retrospect, a neat historical explanation on the happenings of early jazz music in America would be misleading. Oral traditions stress the expressive delivery of their musical substance rather than the compositional integrity upon which they are based. Fascination with the theoretical underpinnings of the jazz expression was a much later development.

AFRICAN INFLUENCES

Music was by far the most vital and demonstrative form of expression in the life of Africans. From morning until night, from the cradle to the grave, everything was done to the rhythm of their music. The art form was passed down by word of mouth from one generation to the next and was a means of preserving tribal traditions, ambitions, and lore.

Music performed a vital role in maintaining the unity of the social group. Singing the same songs in the same way at the same time bound individuals together and established a strong group feeling. Whether religious or secular, improvised or traditional, the music of Africans was a powerful influence in their lives.

In Africa, music was for a whole community, and everyone from youngest to oldest participated. Music was so interwoven with work, play, and social and religious activities that to isolate one phase from its role in the total life of the people is difficult.

The Western European traditional notion of an "art music" tends to place it outside the functional daily workings of a society. For example, classical music is isolated from the lives of average Americans, except in the form of highly structured, well-planned performances. The Africans did not have such a notion of art music—their music was expressively tied to the everyday workings in their lives.

Many of the daily activities within a West African tribe were accompanied by the pulse and beating of a drum. It was a part of religious ceremonies and special occasions such as births, deaths, and weddings. Drums, ranging in size from very small hand drums to great tree drums (sometimes fifteen feet high) were used to frighten wild beasts and to bolster courage in time of emergency. The drum served as one fundamental means of coordinating the movements of the wonderful rhythmic native dances, aided hunting parties, and played an important part in sport and physical exhibitions.

African slaves brought these traditions to the United States and nurtured them in the woe and hardship of slavery. Obviously, the slaves did not intentionally invent a new music at this point; rather, the new music arose unconsciously from the transplantation of the African culture and the African Americans' struggle for survival.

African Rhythms

One common misconception about the origins of jazz is that its rhythms came from Africa. Actually, it is only the *emphasis* on rhythm that can truly be designated African, not the direct influence of any specific rhythmic pattern.[2] Three important points to keep in mind concerning Africans and rhythmic sounds are that (1) religion, very important in the cultures of Africans, is a daily way of life, not just a Sunday activity; (2) African religions are greatly oriented toward ritual—their sincerest form of expression; and (3) African rituals have always involved a great deal of dancing, so rhythmic sounds have always been very important to the lives of Africans.

At the time when the chief exponents of jazz were generically closest to their African ancestry, the rhythms used by these jazz performers were very simple, far removed from the complex pattern combinations used by native Africans. The rhythm used by these early jazz players generally consisted of quarter notes evenly spaced in the measure of music without syncopation or accent. At this time, the very complex African rhythms should have been most influential on their performance!

However, emphasis on rhythm is such a natural element in African life that even African languages are very rhythmically oriented. Because of their rhythmic cultures, Africans were interested in Spanish music. Some researchers even state that Spanish music is so rhythmical mainly because Spain was once conquered by the Moors from North Africa. Thus, it is conceivable that slaves in America heard something from their past in this particular branch of European music. In a pamphlet titled *Afro-American Music,* William Tallmadge writes of African penetration into Spain.

> This penetration occurred during the Mohammedan conquest [758–1492], and accounts for much of the highly individualistic and non-European rhythmic character of Spanish music. Spanish fandangos, tangos, habaneras, etc., were derived from African antecedents. This Spanish music readily amalgamated with the music of the African slaves who were shipped to Latin American countries as early as 1510. Afro-Spanish music influenced the music in North America in two ways: through Spanish possessions in America and through the importation of slaves into America from Spanish colonies. Since New Orleans played such an important part in the early development of jazz, it should be mentioned that Spain controlled that city from 1763 to 1803.
>
> It was soon discovered that slaves adjusted themselves to conditions in North America much better if they were first shipped to the West Indies and acclimatized there before being sent on. Latin American influences have, therefore, been a factor in Afro-American music from earliest times. "Jelly Roll" Morton, a jazz pioneer, once stated that Spanish rhythms were a part of jazz. In connection with that statement one might point out that the traditional bass pattern of [one strain of] the "St. Louis Blues" is a tango. Latin American rhythms continue to exert an influence on the progress of jazz, as these rhythmic patterns are employed in many contemporary styles.[3]

There is no doubt that the Moorish conquest considerably changed the music of Spain, Portugal, and southern France. Therefore, European music brought to the United States had already been influenced by Africa. Many slaves who were brought to America were first kept on the Caribbean islands (which were French or Spanish possessions before they became British) for months and sometimes for years and thus were heavily exposed to French or Spanish music before ever arriving in the United States.

Call and Response

The **call-and-response pattern** heard recurrently in jazz can be traced directly to African tribal traditions. In its original form, the call and response was a ritual in which a leader shouted a cry to which the group responded.[4] A common, present-day form is a congregation's response to a minister or another leader. One hears the influence of the call-and-response pattern constantly in jazz. One example is the musical instance called **trading fours,** in which two improvising instrumentalists play solo parts on alternating four bars. In short, they are responding to each other's musical thoughts.[5] This interplay can be heard on many jazz recordings. Listen to Stanley Turrentine on tenor saxophone and Kenny Burrell on guitar as they use a minor blues tune to go so far as to alternate single measures of improvisation.[6] At one spot in "Casa Loma Stomp," the complete brass and saxophone sections alternate with one measure apiece (NW, 217).[7]

Another example is when a solo instrument "calls" and is then responded to by the background melodic and/or percussive figures of the other members of the band or of a specific section of the band. Listen to the entire band responding to Count Basie's piano in "Queer Street."[8] On the swing part of the CD with this book, the clarinet solo is answered by the trombone section; later, the saxophone section is answered by the brass section. In Manny Albam's "Blues Company," Oliver Nelson and Phil Woods on saxophones are answered by trombones.[9] In Benny Goodman's "King Porter Stomp," Goodman's clarinet has the brass section as a background, whereas the saxophone section is the background for Harry James's trumpet solo. Later in the same selection, the brass and saxes alternate measures.[10]

EUROPEAN INFLUENCES

The melodic feature of jazz is inherited directly from European music. The **diatonic** and **chromatic** scales used in jazz are the same as those used for centuries by European composers.

The harmonic sonorities also derive from European sources: polkas, **quadrilles,** hymns, and marches. This does not dispute the fact that Africans had varying pitches in their drums, reeds, and logs, but the sense of harmony absorbed by jazz is strictly that of the European school.

The African Americans who first sang gospel music, work songs, and so on, satisfied the desire to imitate rich European melody and harmony. On the other hand, nothing in European music could compare with their oral sonority and the rhythmic vitality of their music.

The musical forms of Europe became standard in jazz works. The twelve-bar strains, such as those found in the blues, are directly traceable to very early European music. Most jazz is constructed in a theme-and-variations form that is symmetrical. Africans, however, were not concerned with symmetry of form. In fact, if their music resulted in a symmetrical construction, they considered it crude and unimaginative.

AFRICAN AMERICANS IN THE EARLY COLONIES

The evolution of African music in the colonies depended greatly on the particular colony to which the slaves were brought. In the Latin-Catholic colonies, their musical life was allowed more latitude. Latin planters were not too concerned with the activities of slaves as long as the work was done. Thus, slaves were allowed to play their drums, sing, and dance when not working. The British Protestants, on the other hand, tried to convert the slaves to Christianity. The slaves in these colonies were required to conceal their "pagan" musical inheritance. (It is interesting to speculate on how the resulting music would have sounded if the slaves from Africa had been taken to some part of Asia. For example, if African and Japanese music had influenced each other centuries ago, what would have been the result? Would it resemble any music we know today?)

Congo Square

The name **Congo Square** is frequently mentioned in many accounts of jazz. Congo Square was a large field in New Orleans where slaves were allowed to gather on Sunday to sing, dance, and play their drums in their traditional native manner. (The name was changed to Beauregard Square in 1893. In 1974, plans were finalized for the area to be part of the very impressive Louis Armstrong Park.) The principal significance of Congo Square to the history of jazz is that it gave this original African music a place to be heard, where it "could influence and be influenced by European music."[11] When the famous dances of Congo Square began around 1817, the backgrounds of the participants produced a music that was often a cross between French and Spanish with African rhythms.

CREOLE MUSIC

A segregation movement was initiated about ten years after the end of the Civil War. The **Creoles**—people with Negro and French or Spanish ancestry—were ostracized from white society and joined the ranks of the African Americans. Prior to the segregation movement, the Creoles had the rights and privileges of whites, which included conservatory training for musicians. The combination of the musical talents of conservatory-trained Creoles and the spontaneous oral tradition of African Americans resulted in an interchange of musical expression, and the music that evolved from this assimilation was an early form of jazz.

Most jazz historians leave a considerable gap between the activities at Congo Square and the first known jazz band led by Buddy Bolden at the turn of the twentieth century. Actually, there was no gap because this period was filled by the Creole music in New Orleans. It was natural that this music was mainly French and Spanish and much more advanced (at least by European standards) than the music of the first jazz bands.

There were performances of French and American folk songs, society dances, parades, church music of varying types, and a great plethora of blues singing and playing. French culture was more predominant in the New Orleans area than it seemed to be in any other part of the country. With French culture came the European musical influences heard throughout the territory. In fact, Jelly Roll Morton added his own jazz flavor to much music from the French culture such as operatic excerpts and French quadrilles, one of which he claimed to have transformed into "Tiger Rag."

Social discrimination, as it was practiced in post–Civil War segregation, placed the educated Creoles of French-black heritage into the true American Negro slave society. In 1894, Code 111 forced the Creole to move to the undesirable uptown section of the city. In 1896, "separate-but-equal" status resulted in a closer association of musicians with different backgrounds. Code 111 essentially recognized the distinction between the Creole and Negro but legally declared them equal. This intra-ethnic cohesion reduced status anxiety, and, in turn, helped fuse the disparate cultural influences into a single jazz expression. The Creoles, with their French background, contributed harmonic and formal structures to this early music. Without any directions from the more educated musicians, it would have been impossible for the loosely organized blues or slave music to have congealed enough for Dixieland ensembles to have performed with the great success that was the beginning of this art. A blend of the oral tradition and the European musical tradition was necessary for a successful assimilation by the cross-cultural listening audience of the New Orleans urban society.

> But the repressive segregation laws passed at the turn of the century forced the "light people" into a closer social and economic relationship with the black culture. And it was the connections engendered by this forced merger that produced jazz. The black rhythmic and vocal tradition was translated into an instrumental music which utilized some of the formal techniques of European dance and march music.[12]

FIELD HOLLERS (CRIES)

West Africa had no art music by European standards, only functional music used for work, love, war, ceremonies, or communication. American slaves were often not allowed to talk to one another in the fields while working, but garbled singing was permitted. They established communication between themselves by **field hollers,** or cries, that whites could not understand. The outstanding element of the field cry that is constantly used in jazz is the bending of a tone,[13] which is simply the overexaggerated use of a slide or slur. A tone is bent (slurred) upward to a different tone or pitch, downward to another pitch, upward to no specific tone, or downward to no specific tone. Examples of the four typical ways of employing this feature in jazz follow (for the notation of these examples, see Appendix B):

1. Example 6A demonstrates the bending of a note upward to a specific pitch (demonstration 18 on the accompanying CD-ROM).

Listening Guide

(CD 1, track 1)
Huddie Ledbetter (Leadbelly)—Work Song (Axe Cutting Song)
"Juliana Johnson"*

This song has a two-part phrase structure for each verse. Listen for the accent vocalization on the third beat of each **measure.** This signals when the coordinated work activity would take place.

:00	Verse one, line one. Notice the accent grunt at the end of each phrase.
:07	Second line responds to the first line. The grunts continue on the third beat of each measure, which signals where the axe would fall.
:14	Second verse is a repeat of the first verse.
:25	Third verse. New words: Gonna leave you, (grunt), oh may (grunt) . . .
:36	Fourth verse. Look out Juli, (grunt), oh may (grunt) . . .
:47	Fifth verse. What's a matter with Juli, (grunt), oh may (grunt) . . .
:58	Sixth verse is a repeat of the second verse.
1:07	Ledbetter explains that the singing will continue to show that the rhythm is still maintained, but you won't hear the axes again until later.
1:23	Seventh verse. The singing continues without the accented beats where the axe falls.
1:32	Eighth verse is a repeat of the third verse. Notice that the tempo increases slightly at the end of this verse.
1:41	Ninth verse. I'm gonna get married, oh lord . . .
1:50	Tenth verse. Gonna marry Martha, oh lord . . .
1:58	Eleventh verse. At the end of this verse he says "Axes are coming back now."
2:10	Twelfth verse. Return to verse one with the grunts on beat three.
2:18	Thirteenth verse. Drop them axes, (grunt), oh lord, (grunt) . . .
2:27	Fourteenth verse. Dropping together, (grunt), oh lord, (grunt) . . .
2:35	Return to first verse as the song begins to close.
2:44	Final verse is a repeat of verse three.
2:52	Ends with a final grunt.

*FW1, band 2, Folkways FJ 2801.

2. Example 6B uses a blues cliché to show the bending of a note downward to a specific pitch (demonstration 19).
3. Example 6C illustrates the bending of a note upward to no specific pitch (demonstration 20).
4. Example 6D illustrates the bending of a note downward to no specific pitch (demonstration 21). As it is demonstrated here, this is called a "fall-off." Every jazz fan has heard ensemble endings with this type of bending.

The adaptation of these effects allowed the musician a freedom of embellishment not available in European music.

WORK SONGS

Some African American songs were born on the banks of the Mississippi to the accompaniment of work tasks associated with the riverboats. Others were born in the mines of Virginia, in the cotton fields of the South, and in the labor gangs of prison camps in Texas and Georgia.

The singing of these songs had one thing in common: they were sung without instrumental accompaniment and were associated with a monotonous, regularly recurring physical task. Also, the singing was sprinkled with grunts and groans inspired by the physical effort of straining muscular activity. Many years later, these sounds became a distinguishing feature of both vocal and instrumental jazz.

Jazz historian Rex Harris has described work songs as "tribal songs which started life in West Africa."[14] In addition, he stated that they were used "to ease the monotony of a regular task and to synchronize a word or exclamation with a regularly repeated action."[15] An example of this type of work song is the "Song of the Volga Boatman," probably the best known of all work songs. The grunt indicates the exact time when concerted action is to take place—in this case, when pulling on the oars. (Circus workers standing in a circle hammering huge tent stakes are another example of accomplishing a difficult task through rhythmic coordination; for notation example 7, see Appendix B.)

A good work-song leader was essential in coordinating the workers. He not only caused the work to be more efficiently done but also helped to make time pass. Huddie Ledbetter (Leadbelly) is reputed to have been one of the best leadmen ever, and recordings are available to prove it.[16]

Though work songs varied according to their use, the main contribution of the work song to jazz was the emphasis on rhythm and meter.

MINSTRELS

Minstrel shows were very important in their dissemination of jazz around the turn of the twentieth century. These shows had their beginnings on the plantations: slaves would perform minstrels for the entertainment of the whites; often these performances incorporated true slave songs. The slaves would act in such a way as to mock the whites with their "putting on airs." The whites enjoyed the shows to the point that they themselves put on these same minstrels. The whites would don black makeup and imitate the slaves mocking the whites. The epitome of this situation came about when the African Americans would put on burnt cork black makeup and imitate the whites imitating the African Americans who were mocking the whites.

At the beginning of the twentieth century, traveling minstrel shows were the main form of entertainment for both races. The shows featured the top blues singers of the day such as Bessie Smith, Ma Rainey, and others. The performances were accompanied by small jazz bands, which helped to spread the popularity of the new music.

The cakewalk, a very popular dance at the turn of the century, was often a feature of minstrel shows. It was originally called the Chalk Line Walk in which dancers would walk solemnly along a straight line with buckets of water on their heads. It eventually became an exaggerated parody of white ballroom dancers. It was the first dance to cross over from African American culture to mainstream white society. Contests for cakewalking and ragtime playing became intensely popular and a great moneymaker for Tin Pan Alley.

RELIGIOUS MUSIC

Among the many places from which the jazz expression can be traced, the church is a central contributor. The expressive voices heard there were reflective of those heard in the field, but the subject and much of the musical content is taken from the white spiritual tradition. After the American Revolution, a religious fervor spread throughout this country and expressed itself in revival services and camp meetings. The services offered a marriage of preaching and singing. Most of these meetings were shared, but the congregants were segregated by race. The religious expressions commonly associated with the African American church today grew out of that interaction. The hymns used in these services were of Scottish and English origins as was much of the singing practice. Although much of the musical material was shared, a distinct manner of singing was maintained. The call-and-response technique of African musical groups had a counterpart in Scottish singing tradition of "lining out." The leader sings a line of the hymn and is then joined by the congregation. The resultant sound is one that is comprised of a number of individual and overlapping melodies—individual expressions within the congregation.

This melodic singing style is actually quite similar to that of the African tradition. It is not controlled by the vertical musical structures, meter and harmony, most often associated with Western European music. The rhythm used is freely generated and whatever harmony results is a by-product of the melodic singing style. Such a singing style was accessible to the African Americans who attended the camp meetings. However, the theatrical delivery of the two groups, white and black, did differ. Listen to the Reverend J. M. Gates's sermon

Listening Guide

(CD 1, track 2)
The Reverend J. M. Gates
"Dry Bones" sermon*

:00	Sermon begins.
:09	Spoken responses from the congregation.
:32	Short sung phrases from the congregation.
:45	Hymnlike sung lines in the congregation. This continues off and on throughout the sermon.
:59	Shouted responses to the short phrases in the sermon.
1:06	Gates begins to intone the sermon as the energy of the sermon mounts.
1:27	Shouts from the congregation.
1:33	Gates begins to sing some of the phrases.
1:50	Shouted call and response.
2:13	Gates sings a phrase.
2:32	The sermon's intonation here is very similar to that of a holler.
2:40	Gates begins the main point of the sermon as he continues to sing the sermon. The vocalizations are similar to those also heard in early blues. The congregation continues to respond spontaneously.
3:29	End of the recording.

*Folkways FJ 2801.

"Dry Bones" for both the type of inflections he uses and the manner in which the congregation interacts with him. The call and response used here is spontaneous and the vocalizations suggest later singing styles.

George Pullen Jackson, who authored a great deal of research on the folk music in America after the revolution, suggests that the later, and better-known, black spirituals must be completely attributed to the white spirituals typically used during the Great Awakening. This is certainly an extreme point of view that is generally not supported by other musicologists (see Eileen Southern's *History of Black Music in America*). However, the reciprocal relationship between the two musical expressions and the fact that they shared the same musical context in a common arena is significant.

Church choir
© Bettmann/Corbis

Spirituals

"The impact of Christianity on the African Americans was, of course, the origin of the spiritual; owing to the fact that practically all of the missionary work was done by nonconformist ministers, their evangelical hymns set the style and flavour of the spiritual as we know it today."[17] Around 1800 there occurred in America a religious mass movement known as the Great Awakening. **Spirituals** and revival **hymns** that carried a great amount of emotion were sung at camp meetings. Spirituals, often called "hymns with a beat," were the first original songs created by Protestant African American slaves on American soil.

Spirituals are an excellent example of the blend of African and European cultures and can be easily traced back to 1780, but most seem to have originated between 1790 and 1883. The slaves added their own rhythmic emphasis to any music taught to them, **liturgical** or otherwise. The better-known spirituals of today are the type that were generally heard in large concert halls. Examples are the familiar "Swing Low, Sweet Chariot" and "Nobody Knows the Trouble I've Seen." The European influence of more emphasis on melody and harmony than on rhythm is obvious in these songs.

The greatest number of spirituals performed in the 1800s employed a call-and-response pattern[18] in which there was great emphasis on rhythm, with hand clapping and foot stomping—an example of the West African influence on European liturgy—in a set pattern of emphasis on the second and fourth beats. As Borneman states, "The accent was shifted from the strong to the weak beat."[19] Piano players executed this rhythmic accentuation with the left hand and brought it to ragtime music.

There are many similarities between popular songs and rhythms and religious music in African American church services today. Methodist John Wesley once defended such similarities: "Why should the devil be the only one to make pleasing music?"[20]

> The fervent participation in their "syncopated hymns" is something very remote from the Western conception of reverent quietude as an expression of worship, but hymns without beat are to the Negro religion without God. It is as natural, and no more naive, for them to sing hymns in this style as it was for Renaissance painters to portray Christ in Italian dress and environment.[21]

Early African American church music can be divided into three categories:

1. Many of the selections were improvised, made up at the moment by the preacher and his congregation; they would be remembered and eventually notated. Many of these were based on the blues chord progression because of its simplicity and because it seemed natural and flowing.
2. Some African American congregations would adopt European church music and add not only their own rhythmic concepts but also their own variations.
3. In many cases, African ritual music was altered so that it could be used in these services in America.

The spiritual, besides being a type of folk song, made its contribution to the development of the popular song and to vocal jazz. Although the singing of African Americans attracted little attention in the period before the Civil War, their singing of spirituals began to arouse interest and widespread attention after the war. It is interesting to note that the first collection of American spirituals, *Slave Songs of the United States,*[22] was published in 1867. The collection contains many errors in notation because, in the words of the editors, "their notations could only approximate, not accurately reproduce, the characteristic traits of the music in actual performance."[23]

The singing of spirituals was primarily a group activity performed in a religious setting or on a plantation. There is evidence that spirituals were used in work situations as well. A good example is "Michael, Row the Boat Ashore," one of the songs found in the 1867 collection. Often the song leader would be joined by the chorus singing the refrain (call-and-response pattern).

African Americans also participated in camp meetings, singing the same hymns and revival songs as the whites. In addition, however, they practiced a ceremony after religious services that had a direct influence on the preservation of the spiritual in its traditional performance style. This ceremony, called the "shout" (or "holy dance"), included a group of singers and shouters who would stand to one side singing the spiritual and clapping hands with great fervor while another group would shuffle and dance in a circle with a monotonous thumping of their feet. The swing element in the spiritual was kept alive through this rhythmic intensity of performance.

It is important to recognize the two trends that occurred in the development of spirituals in the middle 1800s. One movement adopted the forms and techniques of European art music, whereas the other conserved the traditional folk character by retaining the characteristics of the African tribal influences. The former spread rapidly through harmonized arrangements sung by choirs and concert performances by trained soloists. The latter, a style much like the shout or holy dance, was cultivated in rural areas or small communities, attracting little attention from outsiders. This type of African American vocal singing used traits that are fundamentally of African origin.

GOSPEL

In 1921, at a convention of African American Baptists, Thomas A. Dorsey was so inspired by the leading gospel singers that he decided to devote his life to the composition and singing of gospel music. His five-hundred-odd songs became so popular that in 1973 he was designated "The Father of Gospel Music" by the publication *Black World*.[24] His composition "There Will Be Peace in the Valley" was written for Mahalia Jackson. He also composed the most popular gospel song of all time, "Precious Lord, Take My Hand."

By 1940, gospel music became so popular in the Holiness churches that these singers were prompted to become professionals and to go on tours. By 1948, Sister Rosetta Tharpe was singing before as many as thirty thousand people in stadiums and parks. She had an unusual ability to raise audiences to new emotional heights through her moaning techniques and shaking head.

In 1950, Mahalia Jackson recorded "Move On Up a Little Higher," and the Ward Singers recorded "Surely, God Is Able." Both sold over a million copies, thus establishing gospel music in the mainstream of American music.

Gospel music, to be better understood, has to be experienced in person. By tradition, when gospel music is performed in African American churches, it is important that the audience respond. In fact, the performer's skill is measured by the amount of active support, or "talking back," that comes from the listeners. Often a singer becomes so caught up in the intensity of the moment that he or she begins to improvise and embellish the melodic lines by bending, sliding, or adding tones, all enhancing the intense feeling generated by mutual emotional release.

Some gospel ensembles consist of groups of men who sing unaccompanied and supply their rhythm by slapping their thighs or hands in time to the music. Other ensembles are composed of women who sing with piano accompaniment and clap their hands for rhythmic accentuation.

The melody of a **gospel song** can be embellished in several ways. These techniques are used mostly by individual soloists or a soloist backed by a vocal ensemble. One of the most popular techniques is to use a passing tone, that is, one inserted between two tones that are a third apart. Another technique is to add one tone either above or below the last tone of the phrase, and yet another is to use several "extra" tones sung in rapid succession either stepwise or by skips.

Gospel singing has been freely adapted by performers of other types of music and is, in a sense, a synthesis of many American vocal styles dating back at least to the Fisk Jubilee Singers. It must be remembered that spirituals and gospel songs are not necessarily musical works of yesterday, as the thoughts and lyrics contained in them are often contemporary. A fine set of recordings (four sides) includes a collection of gospel songs recorded between 1926 and 1968.[25] In fact, gospel and jazz are still partners in vocal groups such as Take 6.[26]

Spirituals sometimes contained symbolic references to the railways or rivers that led to freedom or to heaven, and sometimes the songs gave directions for escaping from slavery. Most spirituals and gospel songs refer to biblical characters such as Daniel, Moses, Joshua, and Gabriel. Many are well-known choral and nonjazz instrumental melodies (e.g., "Nobody Knows the Trouble I've Seen" and "Swing Low, Sweet Chariot"), and others are standard Dixieland and other jazz pieces (e.g., "When the Saints Go Marching In" and "A Closer Walk with Thee").

Gospel songs and spirituals are often considered religious forms of the blues. Blues singer T-Bone Walker agrees:

> Of course, the blues comes a lot from the church, too. The first time I ever heard a boogie-woogie piano was the first time I went to church. That was the Holy Ghost Church in Dallas, Texas. That boogie-woogie was a kind of blues, I guess. Then the preachers used to preach in a bluesy tone sometimes. . . . Lots of people think I'm going to be a preacher when I quit this business because of the way I sing the blues. They say that it sounds like a sermon.
>
> The visitor to a church in Harlem, or on Chicago's South Side, will not find a great contrast to the ecstatic atmosphere that might be found at a jazz concert or in a jazz club. He will find the identical rhythms, the same beat, and the same swing in the music. Frequently, he will find jazz instruments—saxophones, trombones, drums; he will hear boogie-woogie bass lines and blues structures and see enraptured people who beat time with their hands and sometimes even begin to dance.[27]

In the early Catholic churches, participation in the services by even the most faithful worshipers was limited. In the Latin-Catholic colonies, slaves often worshiped a combination of Catholic saints and voodoo deities:

> On the English and Protestant side, the question is as diverse as are the numerous sects of the reformed churches. The Protestant churches are less rigid than the Catholic church; one listens to the sermon and then freely sings hymns. It is this freedom which allows one to celebrate God according to one's own conscience which was to encourage a host of Negroes into the Protestant religions. Furthermore, God, among the Protestants, is praised in everyday language and not in the dead language, Latin. This permitted the Negroes to sing to God according to their hearts and according to some of their own traditions. The ancestral rhythm was reborn, transfiguring a religion.[28]

Methodist hymns were the most emotional, but even these were too somber for the slaves; therefore, improvisation gradually began to creep into hymn singing. "The hymn book of the day stressed part-singing which harmonized only by accident."[29] This accidental vocal harmonization indicates that the voice lines were invented independently of each other. In music, this is known as **polyphonic** (horizontal) construction, and this approach to the creation of musical line was carried over into Dixieland music and was later employed in more contemporary jazz styles. Polyphonic music makes use of two or more melodies that work well together but that also seem independent of one another. By contrast, **homophonic** music is more like singing a harmonizing melody to an existing melody. Both melodies are essentially the same only at different pitches. (For notational examples of polyphonic and homophonic music, see Appendix B.)

Often, some confusion arises regarding the difference between spirituals and gospel songs. Although the two terms are often used interchangeably, gospel songs are usually considered religious songs that recount passages from the scriptures, whereas spirituals are considered hymns.[30]

In 1867, a choral group from Fisk University in Nashville, Tennessee, left school to do a series of concerts to raise money for their college. This group, called the Fisk Jubilee Singers (*jubilee* is another name for a very spirited, joyful hymn), traveled all over the United States, England, and Europe, carrying spirituals, gospel songs, and work songs to an international audience. Examples of this type of singing today are heard in the records of Mahalia Jackson.[31] Generally, most gospel music is very simple in melody and harmony, and the excitement comes from the jazz type of rhythmic pulse.

MAHALIA JACKSON AND THE AFRICAN AMERICAN CHURCH

Gospel music as an art form was all but ignored until the recognition—or, rather, the great triumphs—of Mahalia Jackson. Jackson never performed in a jazz situation, and she sang only songs that she believed served her religious feelings. She believed so profoundly in her religious convictions that she felt entirely free to expose her emotions as sincerely as any singer had ever done.

Francis Ward, writing about Jackson in the *Los Angeles Times*, said, "The earliest important musical influence in her life was blues singer Bessie Smith whose recording of 'Careless Love' was a favorite of Miss Jackson's and from which she learned much about the phrasing of African American folk music. Despite Bessie Smith's influence, Miss Jackson never sang blues or any kind of jazz, only gospel."[32]

For many years, Jackson's singing was not accepted in middle-class African American churches, as her music was a reminder of a lifestyle that parishioners seemed to want to forget. However, record sales grew, and she primed the world for the many gospel singers who eventually followed. Jackson went on to become one of the most stirring, most sought-after singers in the world. She died of heart disease in Chicago on January 27, 1972.

> When a gospel group gets up on stage before an audience, two things become important to them. They want to sing well and to express some religious convictions so that they can reach the souls of the listeners. When the soul of an audience is reached, you will very often see the people shouting, crying, screaming, clapping as a genuine response to the music.

Mahalia Jackson with Louis Armstrong
Courtesy of Les McCann

> Although many Gospel groups write some of their own material, most of the songs making up the repertoires of these singers are old spirituals and religious songs that date back to slavery. These songs have been passed down from generation to generation and the people have sung them in church since early childhood. There are about fifteen or twenty "Gospel standards" that are sung by hundreds of choirs, quartets and groups throughout the country. It is therefore important for a group or singer to create his own sound.[33]

The worldwide penchant for spiritual music has not dampened since the early tours of the Fisk Jubilee Singers, a fact aptly demonstrated by Albert McNeil's Jubilee Singers, who have given concerts to standing ovations in twenty-five countries. Some African American churches today still believe that association with jazz is wicked, an attitude that may account for the lack of African American jazz critics. However, because of the sacred works of Duke Ellington and many other fine jazz composers, this attitude has moderated considerably.[34] In an interview with jazz critic Leonard Feather, singer Vi Redd explained that

> the church was people's only hope in the midst of all the discrimination and oppression, so their ties to it remained very close and they felt obliged to go along with whatever precepts it dictated.
>
> I was brought up in this environment, but not as strictly as some of the other children, perhaps because my father was a musician. Some of the kids I associated with were not even allowed to have a record player in the house. They used to

Marching band in New Orleans
Courtesy of Ray Avery

come over to my place to listen to Nat King Cole Trio records. That was their only opportunity to listen to jazz.

Her [Mahalia Jackson's] music has the same harmonic structure, the same feeling, in many of those gospel songs. By the same token, Milt Jackson is a product of the sanctified church. Sarah Vaughan, Dinah Washington and a lot of the greatest jazz artists came directly out of a church background; yet the people in the church, in all sincerity, still refuse to accept it when it's known as jazz.[35]

MARCHING BANDS

At first, African American music in the United States was vocal, being accompanied by a rhythm of clapping, stomping, and beating on virtually anything available. Then gradually, after the Civil War, African Americans were able to make some instruments and to buy pawned and war surplus instruments. Marching bands began to influence their music. (Military bands, important in all French settlements, also influenced the development of jazz.)

There were many other bands in the New Orleans area as well. Every secret society or fraternity, for example, had its own band, and there were bands for hire that were not affiliated with any organization. Most of the early jazz players started their careers in such bands, playing marches, polkas, quadrilles, and so on.

Vamping

First and Second Lines

When the bands marched down the street, their enthusiasm was enhanced by their "second lines," found in every band. The "first line," or **front line** (not an actual line), was composed of the players of instruments. Those composing the second line were young people who danced and clapped and generally encouraged their heroes in the first line. One of the second line's duties was to carry the instrument cases.

Another, more unusual obligation was to protect the first line from competitive agitators from other bands. Of course, the goal of each member of the second line was to move up to the first line someday.

At the turn of the twentieth century, the most publicized use of marching bands was for funerals. These bands were used not only in New Orleans but also in the Southeast and as far west as Oklahoma. Such bands, usually composed of five or six players, should be considered a separate type of musical aggregation in contrast to large modern bands. Nonetheless, these small marching bands played an important part in the early development of jazz.

For a funeral procession, the African American band would drone a traditional funeral march on the way to the cemetery. After the burial ceremony, the band would march two or three blocks from the cemetery with only a conservative drumbeat. The band would then break into a jazz type of march, such as "Didn't He Ramble" or "When the Saints Go Marching In." The reasoning behind this established plan was that the traditional funeral music elicited mourning, whereas the later use of the more rhythmic music signified that the departed was going to a happier place—a cause for rejoicing.

When the band began to play a livelier version of the march, its followers would gradually respond more to the music. Their responses were often in the form of clapping, stomping, or any physical rhythmic movement leading toward dancing. In those early days, a band often marched directly from the street into a hall, where the same music accompanied dancing.[36]

The most common instrumentation used by these bands consisted of cornet, trombone, clarinet, tuba, banjo, and drums. One of the first leaders of a jazz marching band is thought to have been Buddy Bolden, who is usually credited with establishing the set instrumentation for these bands. Bolden combined brass-band music with ragtime, quadrilles, and blues in the first stages of jazz. The small size of these marching bands made the groups adaptable for various functions such as advertising campaigns, weddings, serenades, and so on. A group might also perform in a horse-drawn wagon, an activity that generated the name **tailgate trombone** to describe how the trombone player sat at the end of the wagon in order to have sufficient room for the trombone slide.

Because this music lent itself so well to dancing, much of the early jazz repertoire developed from marches.

> The transformation of straightforward marches into jazz may be compared with the process which took place when hymns were changed into spirituals. . . . This jazzing of marches was achieved partly by the trick of shifting the accent from the strong to the weak beat and partly by allowing solo players to "decorate" the melody they were playing—solo improvisation; or several players to indulge in their extemporization simultaneously—**collective improvisation.**[37] [Boldface added.]

The regularity of march music could have easily influenced early jazz; today, people often "swing" as they march. The integration of the playing of the conservatory-trained Creoles with the self-taught African Americans produced well-played marches with the freedom of an oral tradition.

Most important to jazz are the emphasis on rhythm taken from African music, the harmonies taken from European music, and the melodies added by the improvisations from American culture. All these elements fuse to make jazz an American music rather than the music solely of the African Americans, who were (and remain) its pioneers and innovators.

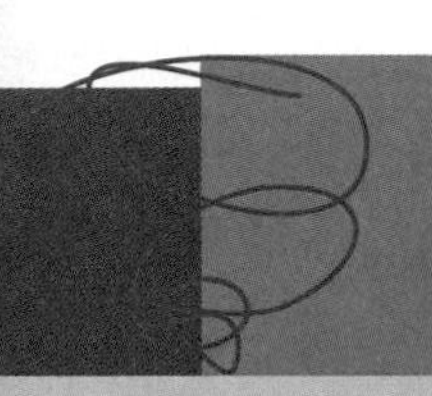

Summary

See Multimedia Companion for additional study materials.

Jazz began with a blending of African and European musical cultures. From Africa came:

1. emphasis on rhythm,
2. call-and-response patterns,
3. expressive interpretive style based on a close relationship between their music and daily living, and
4. improvisational spontaneity typical of oral traditions.

From Western Europe came:

1. the kinds of melodies, harmonies, and musical forms, and
2. compositional approaches typical of literate traditions.

The musical interaction between these cultures can be found in:

1. plantation work songs,
2. church singing (and preaching) styles,
3. minstrel shows,
4. marching bands, and
5. the rich cross-cultural musics of the Creoles in New Orleans.

The balance that jazz strikes between these cultural offerings shifts continuously throughout its march toward art form status. As you will see in future chapters, often new styles emerge whenever the balance shifts dramatically.

FOR FURTHER STUDY

1. American jazz came about through a blend of the musical cultures of Africa and Europe. Discuss the influences on early jazz made by Africans and those made by Europeans.
2. Explain why it is incorrect to say that jazz rhythms came from Africa.
3. Explain the importance of Congo Square and other similar places in the South to the development of jazz.
4. Compare and contrast spiritual songs to gospel songs and to modern liturgical jazz.
5. Describe the following and discuss their contribution to early jazz:
   a. Field hollers
   b. Work songs
   c. Spirituals
   d. Marching bands
6. Give the instrumentation most commonly used in the early marching bands.
7. What is the difference between the construction of homophonic (vertical) harmony and polyphonic (horizontal) harmony?
8. Pretend that you are pounding railroad spikes as you sing the work song "I Got to Roll." Notice the places in the music where the singers give a half-shout or grunt. (This song is found on page 544 of Alan Lomax's *The Folk Songs of North America* [Doubleday], a splendid resource for background material on spirituals, work songs, ballads, and blues.)

ADDITIONAL READING RESOURCES

Brooks, Tilford. *America's Black Musical Heritage.*
Haskins, Jim. *Black Music in America.*
Roach, Hildred. *Black American Music: Past and Present.*
Roberts, John Storm. *Black Music of Two Worlds.*

Note: Complete information, including name of publisher and date of publication, is provided in this book's bibliography.

NOTES

1. B.B. King (b. 1925), U.S. blues guitarist. *Sunday Times* (London, Nov. 4, 1984).
2. "Royal Drums of the Abatusi," *History of Classic Jazz.*
3. William Tallmadge, *Afro-American Music* (Washington, D.C.: Music Educators National Conference, 1957).

4. Ethnic Folkways Library, 01482B, vol. 1, Secular.
5. Santos Brothers, "Beat the Devil," *Jazz for Two Trumpets,* Metro Jazz Records, E1015.
6. Kenny Burrell, "Chittlins Con Carne," *Three Decades of Jazz,* vol. 1.
7. Glen Gray, "Casa Loma Stomp," *The Jazz Story,* vol. 4.
8. Count Basie, "Queer Street," Columbia Records, 36889.
9. Manny Albam, "Blues Company," *The Definitive Jazz Scene,* vol. 2.
10. Benny Goodman, "King Porter Stomp," *The Great Benny Goodman,* Columbia Records, CL-820; *Big Band Jazz,* Smithsonian Collection of Recordings, cassette 3, band 2.
11. Marshall Stearns, *The Story of Jazz* (London: Oxford University Press, 1958), 38.
12. LeRoi Jones, *Blues People* (New York: William Morrow, 1963), 139.
13. "Field Cries or Hollers," Album 8, Library of Congress Recording.
14. Rex Harris, *Jazz* (Baltimore: Penguin Books, 1956), 34.
15. Ibid., 30.
16. *Leadbelly,* Columbia Records, C-30035.
17. Harris, *Jazz,* 47.
18. Stearns, *Story of Jazz,* 93.
19. Ernest Borneman, "The Roots of Jazz," in *Jazz,* ed. Nat Hentoff and Albert J. McCarthy (New York: Holt, Rinehart & Winston, 1959), 17.
20. André Francis, *Jazz* (New York: Grove Press, 1960), 20.
21. Avril Dankworth, *Jazz: An Introduction to Its Musical Basis* (London: Oxford University Press, 1968), 49.
22. William Francis Allan, Charles Pickard Ware, and Lucy McKim Garrison, *Slave Songs of the United States* (New York: Peter Smith, 1867).
23. Gilbert Chase, *America's Music from the Pilgrims to the Present* (New York: McGraw-Hill, 1955), 243.
24. Horace Clarence Boyer, "An Overview: Gospel Music Comes of Age," *Black World* 23, no. 1 (November 1973).
25. *The Gospel Sound,* Columbia Records, KG 31086/KG-31595.
26. Take 6, *Take 6,* Reprise Records, 9 25670-2.
27. Joachim Berendt, *Jazz Book: From New Orleans to Rock and Free Jazz,* trans. Dan Morgenstern (Westport, Conn.: Lawrence Hill, 1975).
28. Francis, *Jazz,* 20.
29. Stearns, *The Story of Jazz,* 63.
30. Francis, *Jazz,* 20.
31. Mahalia Jackson, "If We Ever Needed the Lord Before," *Come On Children, Let's Sing,* Columbia Records, CS8225; *Mahalia Jackson,* Columbia Records, CL 644.
32. Francis Ward, "Mahalia Jackson, Renowned Gospel Singer, Dies at 60," *Los Angeles Times,* 28 January 1972.
33. Charles Hobson, "Gospel," *Sounds and Fury* 1, no. 4 (February 1966): 30.
34. Dave Brubeck, *The Light in the Wilderness,* Decca Records, DX3A-7202; Duke Ellington, *Concert of Sacred Music,* RCA Victor Records, LSP-3582;

Duke Ellington, *Third Sacred Concert,* RCA Victor Records, APL 1-0785; Lalo Schifrin and Paul Horn, *Jazz Suite on the Mass Texts,* RCA Victor Records, LSP-3414.
35. Leonard Feather, "End of the Brainwash Era," *Down Beat* 36, no. 16 (August 1969): 71.
36. Olympia Brass Band of New Orleans, *New Orleans Street Parade,* BASF Recordings, 20678.
37. Harris, *Jazz,* 57.

Singers and Soloists of the Swing Bands, Smithsonian Collection of Recordings.
Sorry But I Can't Take You/Woman's Railroad Blues. Rosetta Records, RR1301.
Washington, Dinah. *Dinah Jams.* Trip Records, TLP-5500.
When Malindy Sings—Jazz Vocalists 1938–1961. New World Records, 295.

ADDITIONAL READING RESOURCES

Albertson, Chris. *Bessie.*
Balliett, Whitney. "Miss Holiday." In *Dinosaurs in the Morning,* 74–80.
Bernstein, Leonard. *The Joy of Music,* 95–111.
Broonzy, William, and Bruynogle, Yannick. *Big Bill Blues.*
Charters, Samuel B. *The Country Blues.*
Chilton, John. *Billie's Blues.*
Harris, Rex. *Jazz,* 34–42.
Hentoff, Nat, and McCarthy, Albert. *Jazz: New Perspectives on the History of Jazz.*
Holiday, Billie, and Duffy, William. *Lady Sings the Blues.*
Jones, LeRoi. *Blues People.*
Keil, Charles. *Urban Blues.*
Oliver, Paul. *Bessie Smith* (King of Jazz Series).
———. *The Meaning of the Blues.*
Pleasants, Henry. *The Great American Popular Singers.*
Smith, Charles Edward. "Billie Holiday." In *The Jazz Makers,* 276–95.
Stearns, Marshall. *The Story of Jazz,* 14, 75–81, 196–98.
Ulanov, Barry. *Handbook of Jazz,* chap. 1.

Note: Complete information, including name of publisher and date of publication, is provided in this book's bibliography.

NOTES

1. Mike Toombs (quoting B. B. King), *San Diego Union,* 11 August 1989, D-4.
2. *Many Faces of the Blues,* Savoy Records, MG12125; Bessie Smith, *Empty Bed Blues,* Columbia Records, G39450; *The Story of the Blues: Jazz Odyssey,* vols. 1–3; Port of Harlem Jazzmen, "Port of Harlem Blues," Albert Ammons, "Boogie Woogie Stomp," Meade Lux Lewis, "Honky Tonk Train Blues," Ed Hall, "Profoundly Blue," Josh White, "Milk Cow Blues," Sidney de Paris, "The Call of the Blues," and Sidney Bechet, "Blue Horizon," *Three Decades of Jazz (1939–1949).*
3. Charlie Parker, "Another Hair Do," *Charlie Parker Memorial/Album,* vol. 1, Savoy Records, MG-12000; Milt Jackson, "Bags' Groove," Horace Silver, "Senior Blues," and Lou Donaldson, "Blues Walk," *Three Decades of Jazz (1949–1959);* Jimmy Smith, "Back at the Chicken Shack," Kenny Burrell, "Chittlins Con Carne," Lee Morgan, "The Sidewinder," and Stanley

Turrentine, "River's Invitation," *Three Decades of Jazz (1959–1969);* McCoy Tyner, "Flapstick Blues," *The Definitive Jazz Scene,* vol. 1.
4. Marshall Stearns, *The Story of Jazz* (London: Oxford University Press, 1958), 15.
5. Leonard Bernstein, *The Joy of Music* (New York: Simon & Schuster, 1959), 109.
6. Rex Harris, *Jazz* (Baltimore: Penguin Books, 1956), 39.
7. André Francis, *Jazz* (New York: Grove Press, 1960), 17.
8. Marshall Stearns, "Sonny Terry and His Blues," in *The Art of Jazz,* ed. Martin T. Williams (London: Oxford University Press, 1959), 9.
9. Charles Keil (quoting Big Bill Broonzy), *Urban Blues* (Chicago: University of Chicago Press, 1966), 37.
10. "Troubled in Mind," words and music by Richard M. Jones. © 1926, 1937 by MCA Music, a division of MCA, Inc. © renewed 1953 and assigned to MCA Music, a division of MCA, Inc. © 1971 by MCA Music, a division of MCA, Inc., 445 Park Ave., New York, N.Y. 10022. Used by permission. All rights reserved.
11. Ralph J. Gleason, "Records," *Rolling Stone* (May 1971), 45.
12. *Ma Rainey,* Milestone Records, M-47021.
13. Bessie Smith, *Empty Bed Blues,* Columbia Records, G39450; *The Empress,* Columbia Records, G30818; *The Bessie Smith Story,* Columbia Records, C1855.
14. Leonard Feather, "Billie Holiday: The Voice of Jazz," *Down Beat* 29, no. 3 (February 1962), 18.
15. *Billie Holiday, The Golden Years,* Columbia Records, C3L-21, C3L-40; *The Billie Holiday Story,* Decca Records, DXSB7161; *Lady Day,* Columbia Records, CL637; *Billie Holiday,* Mainstream Records, s/6000; *Strange Fruit,* Atlantic Records, 1614; *Singers and Soloists, Smithsonian Collection of Recordings.*
16. B. B. King, *Live and Well,* ABC Records, S-6031; *Best of B. B. King,* ABC Recordings, 767.
17. *The Roots of American Music.*
18. Samuel Charters, *The Country Blues* (New York: Doubleday, 1958).
19. Charles Keil, *Urban Blues* (Chicago: University of Chicago Press, 1966); Paul Oliver, *The Meaning of the Blues* (New York: Macmillan, Collier Books, 1960); LeRoi Jones, *Blues People* (New York: William Morrow, 1963).

4

Piano Styles: Ragtime to Boogie-Woogie

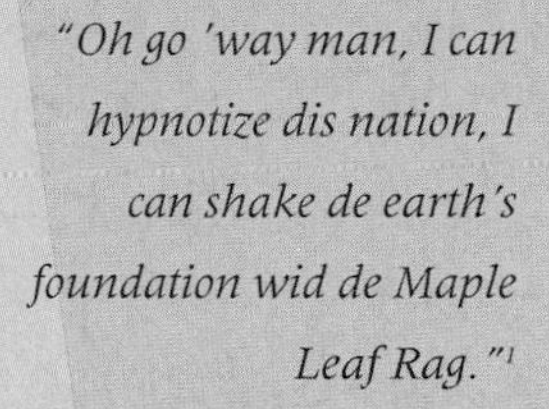

"Oh go 'way man, I can hypnotize dis nation, I can shake de earth's foundation wid de Maple Leaf Rag."[1]

"Maple Leaf Rag" (music by Scott Joplin, lyrics by Sydney Brown)

THE BIRTH OF RAGTIME

Ragtime music has been considered by some to be outside the jazz tradition because it is completely composed before it is performed. But, as was pointed out in Chapter 1, if jazz must be improvised to be considered jazz, then most of the music generally conceded to be jazz could not be classified as such. Even without being improvised, ragtime has the "improvisatory feel" that seems so essential to jazz. On the other hand, some consider ragtime to be another name for early jazz.[2] (For an introduction to ragtime, listen to demonstration 1 on the accompanying CD-ROM.)

Ragtime is often said to have originated in Sedalia, Missouri, because a large number of such players performed there. However, a great deal of ragtime was played before these performers migrated to Sedalia in the late nineteenth century. (When reform government came to Sedalia in 1901, however, all ragtime activity there ceased.) Ragtime, then, predated jazz if Buddy Bolden is considered the one who brought the elements of jazz, or at least of Dixieland jazz, together.

Ragtime had a direct impact on the development of jazz, but because of its juxtaposition chronologically to Early New Orleans Dixieland, ragtime can best be considered a piano style that developed as a result of special conditions.

Because pianists were not used in the first Dixieland bands (which evolved from marching bands), the pianists developed a solo style of playing. A piano player was hired in place of a six- or seven-piece band, forcing the player to develop a technique that provided a full sound. The left hand had to play both the bass notes and the chords, leaving the right hand free for highly syncopated melodic lines. This playing was much more difficult than merely accompanying a vocalist or instrumentalist, in which case a pianist was responsible only for the bass notes with the left hand and the chords with the right. In fact, the extreme

Eubie Blake © Bettmann/Corbis

Demonstration 1
(CD-ROM, track 1)
Ragtime

:00 The first phrase of two choruses of piano solo with tuba, banjo, and drums playing a $\frac{2}{4}$ rhythm accompaniment.

:05 Second 4-measure phrase. Notice the strong upbeat feel on the second and fourth beat of each measure, which is accentuated by the banjo player.

:10 Third 4-measure phrase.

:14 Second chorus. Listen for each phrase and compare the steady rhythm of the accompaniment to the syncopated melodic work.

:28 End.

difficulty of the technique caused many academic piano players to completely oppose the "unusual" style of ragtime. (For notational examples that demonstrate the difficulty of ragtime interpretation, see Appendix B.)

The accompaniment consists of the bass part confined to the first and third beats and the chords played on the second and fourth beats, or **offbeats.** Because of the physical action of the left hand, it became the practice for pianists to accent these offbeats, a technique that led to the new rhythmic style of the following era.

The intricate syncopation used in ragtime compositions could well have been the reason this music was called ragtime, or "ragged time." This is only one of many versions of the origin of the name *ragtime,* and as in the case of the name *jazz,* it is impossible to say which explanation is correct.

Ragtime was a refreshing change from the usual songs that often had commonplace melodies and predictable rhythmic feeling. Unlike many of the blues tunes and some of the spirituals, the mood of ragtime is happy. The country welcomed this happy music because it had just experienced the long depression of the 1890s.

The general public first became aware of ragtime during a series of world's fairs held in Chicago, Omaha, Buffalo, St. Louis, and other cities where peripatetic piano players from the Midwest and the South found employment along the midways. Ragtime flourished for over twenty years. When the music publishing industry (Tin Pan Alley) began to sell "rags," the music was too difficult for uninitiated pianists to play; it had to be considerably simplified if it were to sell. Ragtime players frequently earned substantial income teaching ragtime style.

The ragtime players then began to migrate to Sedalia, Missouri. Though it was later said that ragtime was born in Sedalia, these players merely drifted into the town because of employment opportunities. One player, Tom "Million"

Scott Joplin
Bettmann Archive

Turpin, owned a series of clubs in Sedalia and sponsored many ragtime players. Turpin's "Harlem Rag" (1897) is reputed to be the first rag ever published (although some say William Krell's "Mississippi Rag," also published in 1897, was first). When reform came to Sedalia in 1901, many ragtime players moved to St. Louis, which then became the ragtime center.

Much controversy exists about who composed what rag. Possibly, some rags were a compilation of ideas "borrowed" from many players, and the player who had the knowledge to notate the rag on music manuscript received credit for the composition. It is interesting that typical ragtime selections were composed in a definite format that showed a European influence with its concern for balance and form. Each selection included four themes (or melodies), and each theme had equal stress, or equal importance, within the composition. Examples are "Tiger Rag" and "Maple Leaf Rag." This fairly rigid form was probably borrowed from the construction of marches. Ragtime players, both black and white, were expected to be good readers, and sheet music was one of the principal means of disseminating ragtime music.

Scott Joplin

The most prolific composer of ragtime music was Scott Joplin, a schooled musician who published about fifty rags (some say he composed about six hundred). The most famous, "Maple Leaf Rag" (1899), sold hundreds of thousands of

Listening Guide

(CD 1, track 6)
Scott Joplin (piano)
"Maple Leaf Rag"

:00	A: Establishes the main recognizable theme.
:22	A: Repeat of A forecasts Joplin's involvement with form.
:45	B: New theme demonstrates further attraction to syncopation.
1:06	B: Repeat of the second theme.
1:28	A: Reiteration of the A theme helps the ear hold the form together.
1:50	C: Playing in a higher register causes the third theme to seem brighter in spite of the fact that the tempo stays firm.
2:12	C: Repeat of the third theme.
2:33	D: Syncopation becomes even more daring.
2:54	D: Repeat sounds like improvisation, which of course it is not.
3:17	End.

copies in the first ten years of publication. Many jazz critics are not aware that Joplin wrote a symphony and two operas, one of which, *Treemonisha,* is still performed today.

A monument in honor of Joplin was erected in Sedalia at the site of the old Maple Leaf Club. When the movie *The Sting* was released in 1973, some of the citizens of Sedalia expressed concern about the popularity of ragtime. They were worried that Joplin's tunes would be associated only with the film and that the composer and the city itself would be lost to obscurity. (In hindsight, more recognition could have been given Joplin and his music when he was living there instead of sixty years later.)

Jelly Roll Morton

The best-known ragtime piano player was Jelly Roll Morton (born Ferdinand de Menthe). In his Library of Congress recordings and on his calling card, Morton claims that he originated jazz in 1902 as well as ragtime, swing, and just about everything else in this area of music. He may not have been *that* important, but he was surely at the top among ragtime players. Morton had no peer as a soloist,[3] and he also performed successfully with a variety of bands.[4]

As soon as their finances permitted, some ragtime pianists formed their own orchestras: Jelly Roll Morton formed Jelly Roll Morton and His Red Hot Peppers, Jelly Roll Morton's Stomp Kings, and Jelly Roll Morton's Jazz Band.

Listening Guide

(CD 1, track 7)
Jelly Roll Morton
"Maple Leaf Rag"*

:00	Introduction: driving very hard, influencing a future era to come (swing).
:11	The A strain shows Morton to be a master of syncopation.
:27	Introduction reenters, helping to hold framework together.
:33	B strain as a relief from A, usually called a bridge.
:52	The A strain again but with noticeable additions in both hands.
1:13	Interestingly contrasting section (C).
1:34	Repeat of the C section with new variations.
1:53	New strain (D) vacillates between a tango and a swing feeling.
2:12	Repeat of the D strain, this time in most acceptable stride style.
2:32	End.

*Smithsonian Collection, CD 1, track 2.

Jelly Roll Morton
Courtesy of Ray Avery

Some already established jazz bands then added piano players: Lil' Hardin, later to be Lil' Armstrong, joined King Oliver's orchestra. As the ragtime bands had to have piano players as leaders, this trend carried over to bands not so involved with ragtime. This was especially true in the Southwest, where Bennie Moten, Count Basie, Jay McShann, and many other piano players were leaders.

Morton was an ideal ragtime bandleader. He was an excellent piano player, a creative and knowledgeable **arranger,** and a fair singer. He had an extremely attractive, outgoing personality. In fact, Morton was the first jazz musician who is thought to have precisely planned what each musician was to play on his recordings, thus opening the way for recorded **arrangements** of jazz. The recordings on which he plays piano and talks with folklorist Alan Lomax are important in the history of jazz to the 1930s.[5] "In Jelly Roll Morton, we recognize for the first time in jazz that the personality of the performing musician is more important than the material contributed by the composer."[6] Because ragtime players were becoming bandleaders, the need for players to be more schooled in music became obvious.

RAGTIME AND DIXIELAND MERGE

When the piano players began to play with other instrumentalists, the two music styles, Dixieland and ragtime, began to merge. There are many recorded examples of bands playing rag tunes that were primarily meant to be played on a piano. Listen, for example, to Paul Mares's recording of "Maple Leaf Rag," the New Orleans Rhythm Kings' recording of "Tiger Rag," and others[7] (FJ, vols. 3 and 6).

Two important changes resulted from the merging of Dixieland and ragtime. First, the basic melodic concept of the rags was changed and second, the rhythmic accentuation indigenous to the rags was carried over into Dixieland jazz. As a consequence, a new repertoire was added to the music of the jazz bands, which began to play the rags but altered the form. The first melody became a **verse,** the second and third melodies were omitted completely, and the fourth became a repeated chorus and the basis for improvisation.[8]

The rhythm of the bands changed from a flat four (four equal pulsations in each measure) to a two-four ($\frac{2}{4}$) rhythm (four beats to a measure with accents on beats 2 and 4). These measured offbeats correspond to the action of the left hand of the ragtime pianists.

RAGTIME LIVES ON

Ragtime, then, was a style of solo piano playing that coexisted with Early New Orleans Dixieland jazz. It influenced the interpretation of jazz by shifting the rhythm from a flat $\frac{4}{4}$ to $\frac{2}{4}$ interpretation and by additions to the jazz repertoire, such as "Maple Leaf Rag" and "Tiger Rag."

Ragtime is still played today, and recordings are available from several sources. One source consists of recordings of ragtime played today on a **tack**

piano, which is a piano that is altered to sound much older than it is so that the ragtime sounds more authentic. This is accomplished in various ways. One way is to put thumbtacks in all the felts of the piano hammers. Other ways include laying a light chain across the strings or putting newspaper, aluminum foil, or something similar over the strings.[9] Most of these adjustments, however, are harmful to the piano felts.

Another good ragtime source is the re-pressing of old master recordings by such players as Morton, Joplin, and others[10] (S, "Grandpa's Spells," CD 1, track 8; S, "Dead Man's Blues," CD 1, track 7; S, "Black Bottom Stomp," CD 1, track 6; FJ, vols. 5, 9, and 11). Many good ragtime and stride players made piano rolls that can be purchased, and recordings made from rolls are satisfactory[11] (S, "Maple Leaf Rag," CD 1, track 2).

Another important source consists of recordings of old-timers, such as the two-record set called *The Eighty-Six Years of Eubie Blake,* played by Eubie Blake.[12] Blake, at age ninety-eight, received the Medal of Freedom from President Reagan in October 1981. After charming the nation as a composer and performer for over seventy-five years, James Hubert Blake died on February 12, 1983, at the age of one hundred.

Interest in authentic ragtime began to wane because some players played the style so fast and aggressively that the original relaxed feeling dissipated. As a result, stride playing became more popular. Also, the Dixieland players had destroyed the important ragtime form. Since 1920, however, revivals of this style continue to bring talented composers and players to public notice.

The public was more aware of ragtime in 1973 than during any time since 1920 because of the popular motion picture *The Sting.* Throughout the movie, Scott Joplin's rags established the mood for the period in which the movie was set, and the composer's name once again became a household word. Marvin Hamlisch, the musician who adapted the Joplin rags for the movie, received an Oscar Award for the best movie score of the year. As he accepted the award, Hamlisch acknowledged his absolute indebtedness and gratitude to Scott Joplin and his genius. Joplin (who died frustrated and penniless in 1917) was given screen credits as well.

It is interesting to note that although *The Sting* was set in 1936, ragtime had not been popular since 1920 and that, although ragtime had not been played at all in 1936, the music was still apropos for the movie. It is also interesting that a quiet revival of ragtime had preceded the movie. It was common during 1971 and 1972 to hear students in college practice rooms working on the intricacies of "Maple Leaf Rag." After the release of the film in 1974, students turned their efforts to "The Entertainer," a piece used extensively in the movie. The revival may have preceded the movie, but the film, in turn, strengthened the revival. The important point is that ragtime was once again popular, to the delight of its present-day practitioners.

Ragtime again emerged as the underpinning for the film *Ragtime* in 1981. Both the film and play are based on E. L. Doctorow's novel by the same title. The score, composed by Randy Newman, features a full orchestral setting of several rags, waltzes, and polkas. In 1998, yet another Broadway musical,

"Fats" Waller
Courtesy of Orrin Keepnews

Ragtime, brought ragtime to the forefront of popular entertainment. The music for this play was composed by Stephen Flaherty. Unlike the movie, *The Sting,* which featured a ragtime title song, much of the music of *Ragtime* reflects the syncopation and melodic idioms of the ragtime style, although modernized considerably ("Getting Ready Rag").

At the beginning of this chapter it was mentioned that some authorities do not consider ragtime to be jazz. To illustrate this point, in 1974 the Academy of Recording Arts and Sciences gave an award to a ragtime record without placing it in any specific award category. *The Red Back Book* won a Grammy Award for being the best **chamber music** record of 1973. Its competition included string quartets, classical piano duos, and woodwind trios.

Listen once again to the musical example of ragtime (demonstration 1) on the accompanying CD-ROM (example 2A in Appendix A is the basis of an interpretation showing ragtime style).

(CD 1, track 8)
James P. Johnson
"Carolina Shout"*

Entire selection is a piano solo:

:00	Introduction: 4 bars.
:05	Section A: first chorus—16 bars.
:25	Section A: repeat of first chorus.
:45	Section B: starts out with a vamplike part but develops—16 bars.
1:04	Section C: third type of chorus—16 bars.
1:24	Section C: repeat of section C.
1:45	Section B: improvisation of section B theme—16 bars.
2:01	Section D: new theme—16 bars.
2:20	Repeat of section D theme.
2:39	Coda: 4 bars.
2:24	End.

*Smithsonian Collection, CD 1, track 12.

STRIDE PIANO

As we have seen, jazz bands ignored the original construction of the rags. Piano players were no longer compelled to play alone; consequently, the piano was considered a part of the jazz band's instrumentation. Also, as tempos were increased, the relaxed feeling of the early ragtime gave way to virtuoso displays, and improvisation, not present in early ragtime, began to gain importance in piano music. The culmination of these developments resulted in what is known as stride piano, an extension of ragtime. There are three basic differences between stride piano playing and ragtime:

1. Stride players were not at all concerned with ragtime form. They played popular tunes of the day and any other kind of music that appealed to them.
2. Original ragtime was a composed music, whereas stride players were often very proficient improvisers and used this element in their performance.

Art Tatum
Courtesy of Ray Avery

3. The feeling of stride music was intense because, in general, stride pianists played faster and with much more drive than the more relaxed players of ragtime.

James P. Johnson and "Fats" Waller

James P. Johnson, composer of the famous tune "Charleston" (among many others), is considered to be the father of stride piano. There are many fine recorded examples of his performances[13] (S, "Carolina Shout,"CD 1, track 12; FJ, "Snowy Morning Blues," vol. 9). Closely akin to Johnson, and usually discussed in superlatives, is Willie "The Lion" Smith. However, perhaps the most entertaining and exciting stride piano player was Thomas "Fats" Waller, a student of Johnson. Waller mugged and clowned incessantly; and, if a purist found this disturbing, he merely had to concentrate on the piano playing to hear true artistry and a most energetic rhythmic pulse[14] (S, "I Ain't Got

(CD 1, track 9)
Art Tatum (piano)
"Elegie"

:00	Starts immediately on the original theme.
:11	Repeat and continuation of original theme.
:23	Arpeggio to anticipate personal additions to theme.
:32	Vamp to introduce faster tempo.
:37	Introduction of new harmonic aspects.
:53	Sustained-chord interlude.
:57	Addition of still newer harmonies.
1:05	Trill in left hand and transition into stride style.
1:10	Extended stride style.
1:47	Back to original theme plus Tatum arpeggios.
1:51	Ritard.
2:00	Sounds as if Tatum is about to stop.
2:22	End.

Nobody," CD 2, track 5; FJ, "Handful of Keys," vol. 9; FJ, "Squeeze Me," vol. 11). Waller began to accompany blues singers on recordings in 1922. He was Bessie Smith's accompanist on tour and worked for a short time in Fletcher Henderson's orchestra. In 1927 he formed a solo act. His records sold well, and he even performed in motion pictures.

Art Tatum

Art Tatum was possibly the best—surely the most versatile—piano player in the history of jazz. It is impossible (thankfully) to put Tatum in a stylistic category, but stride was certainly one of his favorites. Tatum worked occasionally with a small group, but he felt this was confining, so he usually played alone. He seemed so far ahead of other players technically and harmonically that he was merely listened to in awe. Tatum was very instrumental in bringing advanced harmonies into jazz. He was almost completely blind, but some maintain that his only handicap was his virtuosic technique—Tatum could not possibly harness his rapid flow of thoughts in order to play with simplicity. Of course, he often proved this wrong. His followers would be Bud Powell, Oscar Peterson, and Paul Smith.

Listening Guide

Demonstration 4
(CD-ROM, track 4)
Boogie-Woogie

:00	First chorus on solo piano (note the left hand is playing 8 beats to the bar while utilizing what is known as the "wagon wheels" pattern); drums play $\frac{8}{8}$ rhythm.
:18	Second chorus.
:36	End.

Art Tatum's recordings include some of the best stride piano on record[15] (S, "Willow Weep for Me," CD 2, track 13). Some musicians never have the opportunity to record their achievements for posterity, but this cannot be said of Tatum. He was hired by Norman Granz for two days of recording in December 1953 and for two days in April 1954. The result was a set of thirteen long-playing records (twenty-six sides) that was released to the public in 1974 on Pablo Records, truly a historic event for Tatum followers in particular and for jazz fans in general.[16]

Another collection of previously unreleased recordings of Tatum received a Grammy Award from the National Academy of Recording Arts and Sciences as the best solo album of 1973.[17] The collection was recorded on a portable home-recording device by a young friend of Tatum's. Some songs were recorded in an apartment and others in various after-hours clubs. The title of the album, *God Is in the House,* was taken from a remark made by Fats Waller when Tatum entered a club where Waller was playing. The remark reveals a respect for Tatum that is common among musicians.

Later Stride Pianists

Oscar Peterson, though also difficult to label stylistically, often ventures into some of the best stride piano on record. He is a talented and versatile musician. Basie and Ellington, too, often went into authentic stride piano during improvisation. Stride can also be heard in an interesting manner in the $\frac{5}{4}$ excursions of Johnny Guarnieri.[18]

BOOGIE-WOOGIE

Boogie-woogie is another stage in the evolution of jazz, and like ragtime is a piano style that was important in the development of jazz. The term *boogie-woogie* itself is very descriptive. Although historically the term is used by Rousas

Vamping

Rent Parties

Rent parties were actually all-night jam sessions. The word was passed around that a musician, or sometimes a friend, could not come up with the rent payment. A piano would be rolled into the apartment, and musicians would drop in and play. On a table would be a hat that acted as a pot for contributions. Much more often than not, when dawn's early light made its appearance, the necessary rent money had accrued. For the musicians, these sessions were often learning experiences, but at times **cutting contests** developed, much to the audiences' approval.

Rushdoony in reference to ancient rites in Morocco,[19] the musical association is the feeling created by playing eight beats to the bar. This style of piano playing came into prominence during an economic crisis—the Great Depression of the early 1930s. Jazz again faced a situation in which a full style of piano playing was needed as a substitute for hiring a band. (For an introduction to boogie-woogie, listen to demonstration 4 on the CD-ROM.)

Ostinato Bass

The most identifying feature of boogie-woogie is the eight beats to a measure that are played as an ostinato, the term for a melodic figure that recurs throughout the music. The ostinato is a structural device that works as a stylistically cohesive element of the composition.

In boogie-woogie piano playing, the ostinato phrase is always in the bass. It is very possible, however, to hear boogie-woogie played by a big band when the ostinato is not present; there will still be eight beats to the bar. Distinguished from jazz played in the even $\frac{4}{4}$ rhythm of Early New Orleans Dixieland or the $\frac{2}{4}$ rhythm of ragtime and Chicago Dixie Style Dixieland, boogie-woogie employs eight beats to the bar in the ostinato.

There are two distinct methods of boogie-woogie playing. In both, the right hand is kept free for melodic interpretation or improvisation. The difference between the two methods occurs in the use of the left hand. In one the left hand plays full, moving chords and in the other a **walking bass** line outlines the chords in a melodic fashion. (For notational examples of these two methods of playing boogie-woogie bass, see example 12 in Appendix B.)

Boogie-woogie has also been called "8 over 4," a description that comes from the eight notes that the left hand of the piano plays in the normal four-beat measure. Although the music might be written in the usual four-beat time signature, the feel of the music emphasizes the eight faster beats. (For notational examples of 8-over-4 playing, see example 13 in Appendix B.)

Meade Lux Lewis
Courtesy of Bob Asen, Metronome Magazine

Although the right hand can play an interesting melodic line, the main feature of this style is rhythmic virtuosity. The left hand and the right hand operate so independently that boogie-woogie often sounds like it is being performed by two pianists instead of one. The style is extremely taxing physically, as it is usually played loudly with tensed muscles, a most tiring means of performing. The **riff** emphasis, typical of Kansas City (to be discussed in Chapter 6), is often heard in the right hand of the boogie-woogie player as the left hand busies itself with the ostinato. Boogie-woogie is generally, but not always, played in the blues form.

The Players

Boogie-woogie was usually played by untrained pianists. Ragtime had incorporated European influences, but it appears as though boogie-woogie piano players worked out their style without any thought of European concert

Listening Guide

(CD 1, track 10)
Meade Lux Lewis (playing)
"Honky Tonk Train Blues"

:00	Piano solo throughout; trill for short introduction.
:02	Chorus 1: left hand playing "full moving chords" pattern, right hand playing melodically and very independently.
:19	Chorus 2: Lewis shows his control by playing 6 beats with the right hand while playing 8 beats with the left (this occurs often on this record).
:36	Chorus 3.
:53	Chorus 4: picks up last small idea from previous chorus and expands on it.
1:10	Chorus 5: uses trills and shows extreme independence of hands.
1:27	Chorus 6: shows a small thought, then develops a technical display.
1:44	Chorus 7: many full chords and use of the "6 against 8" as in chorus 2.
2:02	Chorus 8: similar to chorus 7.
2:19	Chorus 9.
2:36	Chorus 10: getting softer, seems to be tapering down, preparing to stop.
2:57	End.

tradition. Many could not read music, so they simply listened and developed this full style of playing. Most of the time, boogie-woogie players were comfortable playing only this one style of jazz. However, Pete Johnson, who was surely the number one boogie-woogie pianist in Kansas City, was also a fine stride player. He really showed his versatility when he accompanied blues singer Joe Turner hour after hour.[20]

Although it is true that boogie-woogie reached its peak of popularity during the early 1930s, the style surely was not invented then. The first time that the word *boogie* appears to have been used on a record was in 1928 by Chicago's Pine Top Smith as he recorded "Pine Top's Boogie"[21] (NW, 259, side 1, band 4). Huddie Ledbetter claimed that he first heard this type of playing in 1899, Bunk Johnson (an early New Orleans trumpeter) said 1904, Jelly Roll Morton said 1904, and W. C. Handy said 1909. This music has also been called "Western rolling," "fast Western," and "Texas style," indicating that its origin was in the western part of the country, although Florida has also been named as a birthplace.

There were three fairly defined generations of boogie-woogie players. The earlier pianists were active primarily in the 1920s: Jimmy Yancey, Cow Cow Davenport, and Pine Top Smith[22] (NW, 259, Jimmy Yancey, "The Mellow Blues," side 2, band 3; NW, 259, "Tell 'Em About Me," side 2, band 4; FJ, "Yancey Stomp," vol. 10). The middle group, popular during the early 1930s, consisted of Meade Lux Lewis, Albert Ammons, Joe Sullivan, Clarence Lofton, and Pete Johnson[23] (S, "Honky Tonk Train," CD 2, track 6; NW, 259, side 1, band 6; FJ, vols. 9 and 10). The last group included such players as Freddie Slack, Cleo Brown, and Bob Zurke.

Origin

Max Harrison states that this style of piano playing developed from a guitar technique used in mining, logging, and turpentine camps.[24] When three guitar players performed together, one picked out an improvised melody, the second played rhythmic chords, and the third played a bass line. To imitate three guitars at one time, piano players had to develop a very full style by having the right hand play the melodic improvisation and the left hand substitute for the other two guitars. By playing the eight faster notes in the left hand, the piano player can give the impression that the three guitar parts are all there. The result is that both a bass line and the chords are outlined by the left hand, leaving the right hand free to play an improvisation. (For notational examples of how the harmonies are outlined with the left hand, see example 14 in Appendix B.)

Although boogie-woogie is considered a definite piano style, it has been successfully adapted by large bands such as those of Will Bradley, Lionel Hampton, Tommy Dorsey, Count Basie, Harry James, Glenn Miller, and others.[25] The eight beats to the bar created by the ostinato bass is considered its most important feature. This rhythmic component exemplifies the fact that jazz players are always searching for new means of expression. However, having been created within a fairly limited set of circumstances (the guitar origin), regardless of the rhythmic interest, this style's range of expression is not very wide.

Boogie-woogie has never really disappeared, although it is not prominent today. The boogie-woogie revival around 1938 was so popular that almost all performing groups had at least one number in their repertoire. Some boogie-woogie pianists toured and even played in such notable concert venues as Carnegie Hall. Pete Johnson, Meade Lux Lewis, and Albert Ammons perform a boogie-woogie trio on the *Spirituals to Swing* album, which was recorded live at Carnegie Hall.[26] It seems that, when three of these stylistic players perform at the same time, they almost try to outshout one another. In their exuberance they even lose the eight-to-the-bar feeling. The revival was a boon to these players but did not serve to help the style evolve further.

Later Developments

Boogie-woogie laid the groundwork for some later musical styles both inside and outside of jazz. The left-hand rhythm of boogie-woogie is very similar to what later was called "shuffle rhythm." This "shuffle" rhythm was used later by swing groups and imports both the energy and eight-beats-to-the-bar feel of boogie-woogie. The shuffle rhythm was also used by rhythm and blues artists and early rock songwriters like Jim Croce ("Bad, Bad, Leroy Brown").

An even later reemergence of boogie-woogie can be found in the swing revival of the late 1990s, which makes heavy use of the shuffle beat mixed with some rock elements like a heavy backbeat (strong accents on 2 and 4 of the measure). This revival, like the music of the original swing period, was dance centered, featuring the same dances used in the swing period (jitterbug, lindy). Although most of the new swing compositions are original, some revitalized arrangements from the swing period like Glenn Miller's "In the Mood" can be heard at the frequent dance engagements, but these arrangements have a "shuffle rock" underpinning.

Brian Setzer's CD *The Dirty Boogie* is an example of music typical of this swing revival. Although the "jump swing" style of the swing revival often uses some instrumentalists like those in the earlier swing bands, the music reflects its close association with the later rhythm and blues and shuffle rock styles in its dominant use of electric guitar in its arrangements.

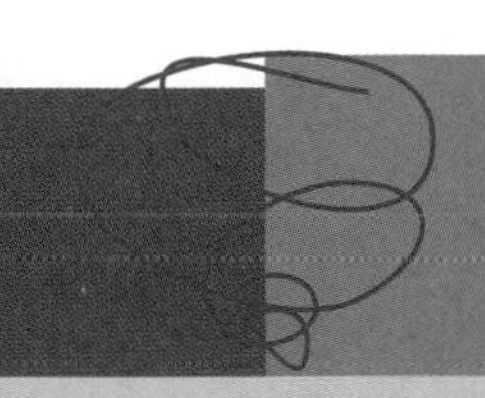

Summary

Ragtime is a composed music played within certain accepted forms that resemble those used in traditional marches. This is not to say that some exponents of this style were not capable of excellent improvisation.

Ragtime displayed a definite separation of the hands at the piano: the left hand played both bass and chords and the right hand the melodic parts. The syncopation in ragtime compositions was advanced for the time, making the music difficult for less proficient pianists.

Stride piano developed directly from ragtime, and it was more aggressive, more improvisational, and less formal.

It appeared for a few years that ragtime was to be relegated to history; however, it is accepted today not only for its nostalgic value but also as regular concert fare.

Boogie-woogie music has not evolved further because, if it were to change rhythmically, it would no longer be considered boogie-woogie. It could progress harmonically, but, because of the very mechanics of performing this style, most players are comfortable only with quite simple harmonies. In fact, since the beginnings of this style, the standard chord sequence has been the blues chord progression, and this is still true today.

See Multimedia Companion for additional study materials.

FOR FURTHER STUDY

1. Compare the musical role of a ragtime pianist with that of a pianist in an instrumental ensemble.
2. How did the techniques of the pianist's left hand (playing alternately bass parts and chords) influence the flat-four rhythm played in early Dixieland music?
3. Listen to "Grandpa's Spells" as played by Jelly Roll Morton (S, CD 1, track 8) and discover the offbeat accents in the left hand. Is this left-hand technique continuous, or does it change at times? If there are changes, what are they?
4. Now listen to "Kansas City Stomp" by Jelly Roll Morton (*The King of New Orleans Jazz,* Dixieland Jazz, RCA Victor, LPM-1649) and compare the ragtime rhythm that Morton used in his piano playing with that used in his instrumental rendition of "Kansas City Stomp."
5. Usually, how many different themes or melodies are there in ragtime compositions?
6. As a result of the merging of ragtime and Dixieland, what happened to ragtime's melodic design and Dixieland's rhythm?
7. What is stride piano?
8. Listen to "Carolina Shout" (S, CD 1, track 12). Is the tempo of the music like a stately march, or is it faster? Listen to the left hand. Is it the "oom-pah" of the earlier ragtime pianists, or is it broken up with irregular, shifting beat patterns?
9. Define the term *boogie-woogie* as applied to piano technique.
10. In this style of piano technique, how many beats are in each measure?
11. Describe two methods of boogie-woogie playing.
12. Listen to "Yancey Stomp" by pianist Jimmy Yancey (FJ, vol. 10).
13. Listen to "Honky Tonk Train" and decide whether the left-hand ostinato bass is in the walking bass style or the chordal bass style.

SUGGESTED ADDITIONAL LISTENING

Boogie-Woogie. Folkways Jazz, vol. 10.
Boogie-Woogie. History of Classic Jazz, vol. 5.
Boogie-Woogie Piano: Original Recordings 1938–40. Columbia Records, KC-32708.
Boogie-Woogie Rarities.
Classic Jazz Piano Styles.
Cuttin' the Boogie. New World Records, 259.
Johnson, James P. *Father of Stride Piano.* Columbia Records, CL 1780.
———. *1917–1921: Rare Piano Rolls,* vol. 1. Biograph Records, 1003Q.
Joplin, Scott. *Joplin.* Biograph Records, 1013/4Q.
Kansas City Piano. Decca Records, DL-9226.

Maple Leaf Rag: Ragtime in Rural America. New World Records.
Morton, Jelly Roll. *The Immortal Jelly Roll Morton.* Milestone Records, MLP 2003.
———. *New Orleans Memories.* Atlantic Records, 2-308.
———. *Stomps and Joys.* RCA Victor Records, LPV-508.
New England Conservatory Ragtime Ensemble. "The Red Back Book," by Gunther Schuller and The New England Conservatory Ragtime Ensemble (playing Scott Joplin music), Angel Records, S-36060.
Pitchin' Boogie. Milestone Records, MLP-2018.
Waller, Fats. *African Ripples.* RCA Victor Records, LPV-562.
———. *1934–1935.* RCA Victor Records, LPV-516.

ADDITIONAL READING RESOURCES

Blesh, Rudi, *Classic Piano Rags.*
Blesh, Rudi, and Janis, Harriet. *They All Played Ragtime.*
Dance, Stanley. *The World of Earl Hines.*
Gammond, Peter. *Scott Joplin and the Ragtime Era.*
Harris, Rex. *Jazz,* 60–72.
Hentoff, Nat, and McCarthy, Albert. *Jazz.*
Hodeir, André. *Jazz: Its Evolution and Essence.*
Kimball, Bob, and Bolcum, Bill. *Reminiscing with Sissle and Blake.*
Kirkeby, Ed. *Ain't Misbehavin': The Story of Fats Waller.*
Rose, Al. *Eubie Blake.*
Shapiro, Nat, and Hentoff, Nat, eds. *The Jazz Makers,* 3–17.
Stearns, Marshall. *The Story of Jazz.*
Ulanov, Barry. *Handbook of Jazz.*
Williams, Martin T., ed. *The Art of Jazz,* 95–108.

Note: Complete information, including name of publisher and date of publication, is provided in this book's bibliography.

NOTES

1. "Maple Leaf Rag" (1903). Music by Scott Joplin, words by Sydney Brown.
2. Guy Waterman, "Ragtime," in *Jazz,* ed. Nat Hentoff and Albert J. McCarthy (New York: Holt, Rinehart & Winston, 1959), 107.
3. *Jelly Roll Morton,* Mainstream Records, S/6020.
4. Jelly Roll Morton, *The King of New Orleans Jazz,* RCA Victor Records, LPM-1649.
5. Jelly Roll Morton, *The Saga of Jelly Roll Morton,* Riverside Records, 9001–9012; *Smithsonian Collection of Classic Jazz.*
6. Joachim Berendt, *Jazz Book: From New Orleans to Rock and Free Jazz,* trans. Dan Morgenstern (Westport, Conn.: Lawrence Hill, 1975).

7. Paul Mares, "Maple Leaf Rag," *Folkways Jazz,* vol. 6; New Orleans Rhythm Kings, "Tiger Rag," *Folkways Jazz,* vol. 3; Joe King Oliver, "Snake Rag," *Folkways Jazz,* vol. 3; New Orleans Feetwarmers, "Maple Leaf Rag," *Folkways Jazz,* vol. 11; Papa Celestin, "Original Tuxedo Rag," *Jazz Odyssey,* vol. 1.
8. Waterman, "Ragtime," *Jazz,* 7.
9. Phil Moody, *Razz-Ma-Tazz,* Urania Records, UR 9009; Joshua Rifkin, *Scott Joplin Ragtime,* Nonesuch Records, H-71248.
10. Jelly Roll Morton, "Grandpa's Spells," *Piano Roll Hall of Fame;* "Perfect Rag," *History of Classic Jazz,* vol. 2; "Big Fat Ham" and "Black Bottom Stomp," *Folkways Jazz,* vol. 5; "Tom Cat Blues" and "Wolverine Blues," *Folkways Jazz,* vol. 9; "Kansas City Stomps," *Folkways Jazz,* vol. 11; "London Blues," *Jazz Odyssey,* vol. 1; "Someday Sweetheart," *Jazz Odyssey,* vol. 2; Scott Joplin, "The Cascades," *History of Classic Jazz,* vol. 2; "Original Rags," *Folkways Jazz,* vol. 11; *History of Classic Jazz,* vol. 2; *The Jazz Story,* vol. 2; *Reunion in Ragtime,* Stereoddities Records, S/1900.
11. *Piano Roll Hall of Fame* and *Piano Roll Ragtime,* Sounds Records, 1201; Jelly Roll Morton, *Rare Piano Rolls,* Biograph Records, 1004Q; Fats Waller, *Rare Piano Rolls,* vols. 1 and 2, Biograph Records, 1002Q, 1005Q.
12. Eubie Blake, *The Eighty-Six Years of Eubie Blake,* Columbia Records, C2S-847.
13. James P. Johnson, "Keep off the Grass," *Jazz Odyssey,* vol. 3; "Black Bottom Dance" and "Mr. Freddie Blues," *Piano Roll Hall of Fame.*
14. Fats Waller, *Ain't Misbehavin',* RCA Victor Records, LPM-1246; "Mama's Got the Blues," *History of Classic Jazz,* vol. 8; "Handful of Keys," *Folkways Jazz,* vol. 11; "Draggin' My Poor Heart Around," *Jazz Odyssey,* vol. 11; "Do It Mr. So-and-So" and "If I Could Be with You," *Piano Roll Hall of Fame;* "The Flat Foot Floogie," *The Jazz Story,* vol. 3; *The Complete Fats Waller,* Bluebird Records, 2AXM-5511.
15. Art Tatum, *The Art of Tatum,* Decca Records, DL 8715; *Piano Discoveries,* vols. 1 and 2, 20th Fox Records, Fox 3032/3; "Too Marvelous for Words," *Smithsonian Collection of Classic Jazz.*
16. *The Tatum Solo Masterpieces,* Pablo Recordings, 2625 703.
17. Art Tatum, *God Is in the House,* Onyx Recordings, ORI 205.
18. Johnny Guarnieri, *Breakthrough in 5/4,* Bet Records, BLPS-1000.
19. Rousas J. Rushdoony, *The Politics of Pornography* (Sandtron City, Sandtron, South Africa: Valiant Publishers, 1975), 98.
20. Joe Turner and Pete Johnson, "Roll 'Em Pete," Columbia Records 35959; "Johnson and Turner Blues," *Jazz of Two Decades,* EmArcy Records, DEM-2.
21. Pine Top Smith, "Pine Top's Boogie," *Encyclopedia of Jazz on Records,* vol. 1.
22. Jimmy Yancey, "The Fives," *History of Classic Jazz,* vol. 5.
23. Meade Lux Lewis, "Far Ago Blues," *History of Classic Jazz,* vol. 5; Albert Ammons, "St. Louis Blues," *Folkways Jazz,* vol. 10; Joe Sullivan, "Little Rock Getaway," *Folkways Jazz,* vol. 9; Clarence Lofton, "Brown Skin Gal," *Folkways Jazz,* vol. 10; "Blue Boogie," *History of Classic Jazz,* vol. 5; Pete Johnson, "Let 'Em Jump," *Folkways Jazz,* vol. 10; "Lone Star Blues," *History of Classic Jazz,* vol. 5.

24. Max Harrison, "Boogie Woogie," in *Jazz*, ed. Nat Hentoff and Albert McCarthy (New York: Holt, Rinehart & Winston, 1959), 107.
25. Will Bradley, "Beat Me Daddy, Eight to the Bar," Columbia Records, 35530; Lionel Hampton, "Hamp's Boogie Woogie," Decca Records, 71828; Tommy Dorsey, "Boogie-Woogie," RCA Victor Records, 26054; Count Basie, "Boogie-Woogie," *The Best of Basie*, Roulette Records, RE118; Harry James, "Boo Woo," Columbia Records, 35958; Glenn Miller, "Bugle Woogie," *The Glenn Miller Chesterfield Shows*, RCA Victor Records, LSP-3981 (e).
26. Pete Johnson, Albert Ammons, and Meade Lux Lewis, "Cavalcade of Boogie," *From Spirituals to Swing*, Vanguard Records, VRS-8523/4.